DATE DUE

			PRINTED IN U.S.A.

COLLAGE

Pasted, Cut, and Torn Papers

COLLAGE
Pasted, Cut, and Torn Papers

by

Florian Rodari

SKIRA

RIZZOLI
NEW YORK

Reproduction rights reserved by PRO LITTERIS, Zurich,
and Cosmopress, Geneva

Published in the United States of America in 1988 by

Rizzoli INTERNATIONAL PUBLICATIONS, INC.
597 Fifth Avenue/New York :0017

Translated from the French by Michael Taylor

Printed in Switzerland

Library of Congress Cataloging-in-Publication Data

Rodari, Florian.
   [Collage. English]
   Collage: pasted, cut, and torn papers / by Florian Rodari.
     p. cm.
   Translation of: Le collage.
   Bibliography: p.
   ISBN 0-8478-0961-7: $75.00
   1. Collage — Technique.   I. Title.
N7433.7.R6313 1988
702'.8'12 — dc 19

88-6641
CIP

CONTENTS

Pablo Picasso
(1881-1973)
Sheet of Music and Guitar, winter 1912-1913.
Pinned and pasted papers.

INTRODUCTION

The art historian, and the art lover in general, can learn as much from study-ing the "secrets" of picture making that define an artist's manner as from mastering the different external movements and historical and social factors that influence a work of art at one stage or another. Every time we try to "read" a work of art we ought to take certain precautions. We ought to acquaint ourselves with the specific properties of the technique employed by the artist. We ought to try and understand the reasons why the artist chose to use it. We ought to measure its strengths and limitations. In a word, we ought to try and understand its "physiology," if only because this involves the pleasure of looking at art.

None of this can be undertaken, however, unless scholars agree about influences and dates; unless there is a consensus about interpretations and a general acceptance of the fact that the perceptual order expressed in a painting is not the order of external reality and that art and the world, notwithstanding the mirrors they hold up to each other, will never intersect. Only once we have returned to an elemental nakedness and silence will we be able to connect our emotion to the actual terms of art's irreplaceable reality: the sign-writing of "forms and colours assembled in a certain order" (to paraphrase Maurice Denis) which is, as we will see, the single issue at stake in the interchange between the eye and the work shaped in the flames of visual desire.

My intention is not to formulate rules or to enter into the details of exact, often complex studio practices that in final analysis belong to the artist alone. My task here is a more urgent one. I want to remind the reader that the choice of materials in a work of art, the fact that the artist elects to utilize certain physical properties of those materials (properties discernible even to an untrained eye) and chooses to employ certain instruments and formal structures rather than others, inevitably have a bearing on the way we read a work of art. They determine its spatial and temporal dimensions to the same extent, if not more so, than do the choice of subject and the histor-ical context (which offer only a secondary explanation of the work's uniqueness).

The fact is that an artist does not select one procedure in preference to another unless there is a profound affinity between his desire and the physical properties of the technique he uses. Put in more concrete terms, it is the artist's respect for the requirements of the medium he works in, his hand's efforts to bend a resistant material to the dictates of his heart and mind (in the process sometimes discovering hitherto unexplored resources), that give his work its uniqueness.

Each of the techniques available to the artist contains a number of measurable data, of potential gestures, of authorized reactions which translate with varying degrees of naturalness the emotion that gave birth to the work or the involvement that sustains its creation. Certain physical characteristics of the watercolour technique, for example, make it ideally suited to render changes of outdoor light and atmosphere. The balance between dry powder and gum in pastels is perfect for expressing the fine texture of skin and the nap of fabrics. Engraving, which forever secretes the dark ink of melancholia, like oil painting (another slow, complex technique demanding an awesome technical expertise), has long served a carefully controlled view of the world.

As for collage, it seems especially suited to express art's questioning and self-questioning spirit. More than any other technique, it can render visible, or more exactly isolate, the formal means of image making. Stressing the breaks and discontinuities between its different components, the collage of cut-out, torn, or, simply, "found" fragments seems to split up the act of seeing itself. For centuries artists were content to *see*, to fondle things promiscuously with their eyes. They gave little thought to the complex interchange between visible signs, the retina, and the nerve connections that communicate perceptions to the brain, which organizes them into a visual coherence. Suddenly, at the beginning of the twentieth century, this process seemed of vital interest to painters. The first pasted paper transformed the smooth surface of the picture (that window looking out on the world, that arena of pictorial mimesis) into a radically new field of experimentation: it revealed seams and thicknesses; it displayed the crude mechanics of picture making; it gave prominence to reliefs and hitherto unrecognized shadows; it amplified tactile perceptions. By thus introducing actual materials into the picture, artists offered fresh insight into its inner workings, *showing it up from within.*

This conscious exposure, which the artist arrived at by analyzing the vocabulary and syntax of his own mode of expression, initiated a new set of relations between his eye and the world, relations which radically inverted the comprehension of art. From then on, it was the artist's very gesture as he executed the work which was "brought forth on to the terrain of contemplative purposes" (Lévi-Strauss). Reflecting the artist's impatience with the visible world, meanings hidden beneath the obvious were combined with an impulsiveness, a creative randomness liberated from the dead weight of conventions. They wedded the medium's specific properties (its textures, its interacting unmixed colours and elementary forms) and active compositional structures to create a spectacular insurrection on the picture plane. Under the chaotic impact of collaged fragments, of pressures thrusting upwards, the surface buckled, split open, and spilled into actual space. Gone was the easy urbanity of the past. Instead of leading the spectator's eye on towards an unattainable distance, the pasted paper traps it in concreteness. It celebrates materials, substances, textures. It brings the artist's actions and the interaction of forms into visibility. It designates clearly what is actually at issue in the work and in the work's space: the here and now where life dances, so to speak. Confronted with collage's startling rhythms, with *non sequiturs* and nonchalant elisions that jar our visual habits and baffle our rational mind, confronted too with drastic shifts and distortions of space, we are obliged to abandon the old system of the single viewpoint and the virtually unbroken temporal continuum. Thrust into the very centre of the work, we participate in its creation. We reconstruct it with our own hands, as it were. By identifying closely with its plastic requirements we can hope to discover its secret.

This twofold process combines intellectual analysis with perceptual feeling. (Similarly, the architect's flights are based on the engineer's blueprint, the poet's innovations rest on the grammarian's rules.) This is why some critics have stated that with the advent of collage, painting at last returned to the realm of the intellect. It regained the rigorousness of a *cosa mentale* after having been dissolved in the fortuitousness of "*la petite sensation.*" The point s that while a work of art needs to be fecundated by the viewer's eyes, the eye itself remains inoperative until it recognizes a supreme coherence in the formal elements and in the syntax that organizes them in such a way as to declare the prestigious autonomy of art.

PART ONE

THE PASTED PAPER REVOLUTION

The amazement which greeted the sudden appearance of the pasted paper in the field of classical figuration and the speed with which this practice spread between 1912, the date of its "revelation" to Braque and Picasso, and 1925, when it began to be widely accepted, is eloquent proof that the pasted paper revolution was one of the crucial phases of modernity in art. As early as the years just mentioned the procedure of borrowing elements from reality (manufactured items, quotations from printed illustrations, discarded scraps, and even bits of waste) and including them as is in works of art helped significantly to transform prevailing modes of seeing and feeling. Whether it was conceived as a weapon or as an object of fancy, the real material now began to play a tangible role in the viewer's perception of the work. It spoke simultaneously to his mind and to his sense of touch; it brought art and life closer together.

The radical nature of the revolution in the traditional system of pictorial representation ushered in by the pasted paper was not recognized right away by art historians. (Poets were faster to discern its significance: first Apollinaire, then Breton, Aragon, Tzara, and later Jean Paulhan.) But the diversity of uses to which it was put by the numerous meteoric avant-gardes of the early part of this century reflects both the richness and the requisiteness of this novel language. The invention of collage has often been compared to the development of the perspective system in painting towards the beginning of the Renaissance. Alberti's definition of two-dimensionally rendered space was the culmination of a whole series of empirical experiments and clumsy attempts to depict recession. It thus brought a theoretical confirmation to the gropings of those precursors who had struggled intuitively to show the world in terms of depth. The almost accidental discovery of collage likewise confirmed countless probings and reflections on the requisite conditions for a new pictorial syntax; at the same time it allowed this syntax to express itself freely and fully. And so, like the optical system that Alberti devised in the fifteenth century, this revolutionary technique was simultaneously the agent of a new vision and the means by which that vision was manifested—and this at the precise point when that vision was coming into existence.

Pablo Picasso
(1881-1973)
Still Life with Chair Caning, May 1912.
Oil, oilcloth and paper on canvas surrounded by rope.

Yet the act of pasting was a direct assault on the system of privileges established by perspectivist theory. It replaced the single viewpoint with an optical plurality that shattered the logical continuity of the spatial illusion at every point. Moreover, it made a mockery of the idealist traditions that had come to be associated with the practice of art since the Renaissance. Not only was it an artisanal technique; not only did it suddenly open up artistic endeavour to materials that had formerly been relegated to the applied and popular arts: wallpapers, typographic vignettes, newspapers, scraps of ribbon, rope, fabric, bits of wood, glass, iron, stone, and even concrete—in short, all manner of materials that were utterly alien to the sacrosanct canons of Art

with a capital A. But, what was more, the very process of cutting out, pasting, and assembling fragments (a process that had up until then been confined to the fields of engineering and industrial production) began to compete with the subjective refinement and the sovereign personality of the artist, which had long been recognized as his exclusive privileges, the hallmarks of his genius.

Within a few years, illusionism with its counterfeit reality, its voiceless remains, its intrigues, its oversubtle distinctions, was retreating on every front. On a scene stripped bare of glitter and symbolic clutter, a team of constructor-artists wielding tools was instead displaying the secrets of their trade with a joyous openness. Everywhere a fresh, breathless poetics was cracking the husk of conventional and commonplace meanings and releasing the plain beauty of things in their pristine immediacy. A clumsy spontaneity was edging out the old standards of skill. The ideal models that were products of patience and a technical expertise transmitted by academies were being set aside for crudely cut-out and roughly assembled objects. In this redefined aesthetic geography, the artist's hand was getting its rhythms from machines; and machines with their set motions and revolving interlocking gears were suggesting new combinations to the artist, combinations that revealed the dynamics inherent to the work. Under the impact of these changes music scores were beginning to register the noise of motors, the clickings of automatons, the grindings, stridencies, loud clangs, and detonation of the modern aural landscape. In the theatre, the spectator was being allowed to look into the wings at the secrets of stage machinery: the levers, chains, and pulleys. Faster rhythms were making their appearance in choreography; dancers were donning costumes made of cardboard, wood, and aluminium. The mannequin with its clearly visible articulations and its implausible positions was becoming an emblematic figure of the new sensibility, the new fascination with the hidden forces governing our daytime actions. Thanks to this resurgence of vitality, the primitive art of remote and little-known peoples was being hailed as a salutary return to sources after the formal ponderousness of academicism. Popular expressions, quotations in foreign languages, fast technical jargon, were entering the stuffy precincts of literature, flouting etiquette, and releasing energies that had long been lying dormant. Amid this flurry of radical innovations books too were beginning to change. They were losing their bulkiness and heaviness; they were coming down from the shelves of private libraries and were now of a size to be carried in pockets. Hastily printed on inexpensive

Ivan Puni
(1892-1956)
Suprematist Sculpture, 1914.
Wood, sheet iron, cardboard, paper, gouache.

Francis Picabia
(1879-1953)
Flower Pot, c. 1925.
Oil and object collage on canvas.

FRANCIS PICABIA

paper and limited more often than not to a handful of copies, they were making up for their fragility and slenderness with an abundance of plastic solutions that continues to amaze us today. They are indeed wonderfully indifferent to set distinctions between genres, these portable laboratories where poetry and painting seem to be working out new ways of relating, where both the hand and the eye are engaged in the pleasure of reading. They combine such widely different techniques, techniques that seem to have been improvised under the pressure of limited time and means. Writing and a typography emancipated from the rigid order of the compositor's tray are constantly being helped along by the artist's imagination. Inventive layouts, remarkably responsive to the urgings of the new aesthetic, break up the flow of the printed text; while the interaction of the different materials and the action of folding, assembling, and pasting remind the reader engaged in contemplating a single page or in thumbing through the volume that the book has its own truth as an object made of equal parts of space and time.

The instant success of collage among all the artists who were involved in renewing forms and ideas in the first decades of this century shows clearly that it was more than just a mechanical procedure or a new man-

ual technique. More than just a practice, it was in fact a principle; one that served as a support for every kind of technique; one that enhanced every mode of expression, whether visual, musical, or literary. In every field it seemed by far the best weapon for conducting the revolution against the old order; the best instrument for placing the perennial values of art into question; the most effective tool for breaking down what was now held to be the illusory coherence of traditional works and for replacing idealist intentions with the rough, independent, openly declared signs of painting. These signs in some cases stressed picture making and determined the essential conditions of the image's sudden emergence; in other cases they commented ironically on the permanence of the image, or they amplified its shock value. From the outset, collage was simultaneously the medium and the object of a lucid meditation on the meaning of artistic activity and its real stakes. Under its seditious influence, the frame's limits were burst; the picture surface buckled into three-dimensional space; the distinctions that had hitherto kept genres separate collapsed. Finally, the old norms of unity (whether spatial or temporal), harmony, and taste, and the traditional standards of slow polished craftsmanship, gave way to new criteria: discontinuity, mixed media, "ugliness" as an

Kurt Schwitters
(1887-1948)
Merz Construction (Merzbau) in the artist's home,
Hanover, c. 1923-1933.
Assemblage, destroyed in 1943.

14

expressive value, wit, speed, and incompleteness. The associative rhetoric of collage achieved its effects through violent, startling contrasts, accumulations, substitutions, divulgations, metaphors, verbal and visual puns. It was used successively in the Cubist venture to redefine pictorial space, the Suprematist experiments with the textures and formal elements that constitute the very essence of painting, the Dada assault on established values, and the Surrealist program of tunnelling into the unconscious and tapping its precious veins.

From the very first moment of its appearance, collage seemed to promise unlimited possibilities. Picasso began to make three-dimensional objects, musical instruments, and still lifes around the time he executed his first collage (the *Still Life with Chair Caning*), even before his experiments with pasted paper on canvas. These constructions consisted of bits of cardboard, scrap wood, and iron fastened together with glue, screws, nails. Starting with the sheet metal *Guitar* of May 1912 he elaborated a hitherto unknown art of assemblage that was destined to become increasingly successful. It was characterized by constructions of planes that were cut out and fastened together so that their surfaces—coloured painterly surfaces—unfold in three-dimensional space. These works were followed by ambiguous reliefs like Ivan Puni's *Suprematist Sculpture* (1914) which combine the abstract forms of pictorial representation with concrete, tangible materials: they seem to hesitate between mural frontality and the multiple viewpoints of sculpture. While some artists opted for collage because of its innumerable plastic and spatial possibilities, others speedily adopted it to the exclusion of all other techniques for its iconoclastic potential. The latter is true of all the Dada artists, who employed collage to question the very existence of painting in object-pictures, photomontages, and prototypic "accumulations" that jibed at tradition with increasing insolence. Picabia, for example, singles out the futility of all artistic striving by replacing line and colour in his banal *Flower Pot* dating from about 1925 with the tools (brushes, cups, and palette) of their triumph on canvas in the past.

In some cases, whole works were contrived with the help of glue, nails, or cement. The indefatigable Kurt Schwitters spent his entire career collecting, sorting, and assembling bits of waste from the contemporary urban environment. He made three different attempts at constructing a *Merzbau,* a sort of private temple or "Cathedral of erotic misery" in which all the fragments of reality he collected were preserved in plaster—literally collage applied to architecture. Other artists ex-

pressed random encounters, the choice of primitive spontaneity over logic and conscious intention, by accumulating composite elements in novel, unclassifiable works; visual meditations in the form of conundrums or dreams; provocative objects whose sole function is to unlock the gates of reality and confront us with new riddles. Man Ray's assemblage of paraphernalia in *For Writing a Poem With* (1923) is a good example of this.

Giorgio de Chirico
(1888-1978)
The Melancholy of Departure, 1916.
Oil on canvas.

Collage and assemblage exerted such a strong fascination at this time that some artists acknowledged its influence even though they did not actually use it as a technique. In Chirico's pictures the collage method is translated into paint on canvas by a strictly mental process assembling disturbing images without resorting to paste. The Surrealist aesthetic is based on precisely this type of rhetoric, a rhetoric characterized by the imagination using, and indeed often abusing, possibilities suggested by associating disparate beings or realities. In the *Melancholy of Departure* (1916) inconsistent lines of perspective and incongruous planes short-circuit logic to produce a sense of contradictoriness and estrangement which detonates a powerful poetic charge in the viewer's mind. The same principle underlies Magritte's entire output. Except for the actual physical act of painting, which remains classical, if not academic, the spirit of his art is wholly that of collage. His *Comic Spirit* (1927), symbolized by a cut-out paper figurine, a useless blind puppet, masterfully expresses the perils of a painting which is based chiefly on brain-waves and flashes of wit.

But the artist who went farthest and showed the finest sensitivity in analyzing the new set of conditions created by the invention of collage was Marcel Duchamp. At several points in his always deeply meditated production he used the collage principle to substitute a concept for an actual work; to transform through an arbitrary yet supreme mental act a trivial

Marcel Duchamp
(1887-1968)
In Advance of the Broken Arm, 1915.
Readymade (snow shovel).

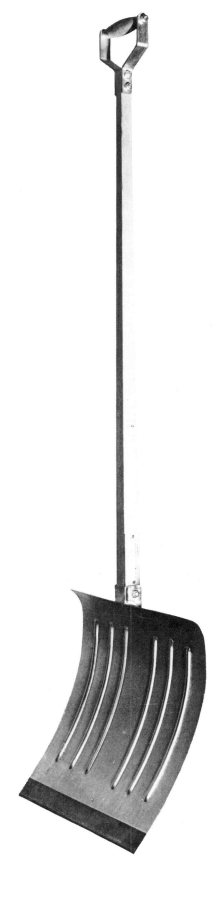

and banal reality into the reality of art; and, literally, to affix an aesthetic "label" on some ordinary object—a snow shovel or bottle rack—that otherwise has none of the prerequisites of a work of art.

As early as 1914, Duchamp extended the pasted paper's range of possibilities to its ultimate expression with the invention of the Readymade. The manufactured item was now no longer just a fragment within the work; it *was* the work. Art, declared this adept of paradox, no longer resided in the essentially relative personal tastes of the artist, but in an anonymous minimal gesture vested in a deliberate intellectual choice, one that, in the eyes of the spectator, restores the primacy of the artistic act.

"It is the spectator who makes the picture," declared this uncompromising indolent aesthete who found a way, with the Readymade, to create a work effortlessly, thus anticipating by some fifteen years Aragon's prediction in his important essay *La Peinture au défi* (1930) that "a time will come when painters, who have already given up preparing paints, will consider it childish and unworthy to spread paint themselves. . .they won't even employ others to do it for them; they will even cease drawing. Collage gives us a foretaste of that time."

It seems unlikely that the Surrealist poet's prediction will ever come true. Nevertheless one cannot help but notice how influential the concept of collage and how widespread the practice of collage has become in contemporary art.

It is impossible to overlook the fact that from the outset, collage acted as a fresh and liberating stimulus. Unlike classical techniques such as pastel and watercolour, it challenged all set limits. It could not be reduced to an ordinary plastic language. It began immediately to function like a "machine for seeing," to borrow Jean Paulhan's apt expression—and soon even like a machine for meditating. Its influence spread rapidly to all the visual arts: painting, sculpture, architecture, as well as the theatre, the movies, photography, advertising, and book publishing. It pushed back their boundaries, sped up their rhythms, set their traditional prerogatives into play in new ways, and lent itself to exchanges and crosscurrents that proved fruitful to all the arts.

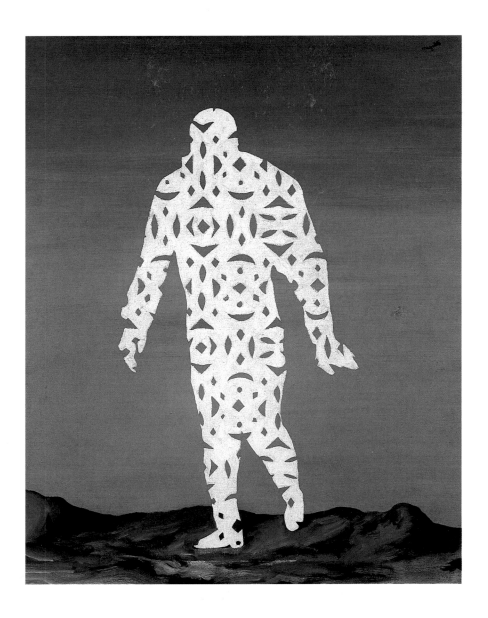

René Magritte
(1898-1967)
The Comic Spirit, 1927.
Oil on canvas.

What is more, collage's ability to transgress traditional lines of demarcation and its capacity for invention have marked a number of contemporary art movements, such as American combine painting, Pop Art, Happenings, environments, New Realism, conceptual art, Arte Povera, and so forth.

Although this broad range of approaches and practices is inseparable from the overall history of collage in the twentieth century, it nevertheless presents a danger for art historians: that of lumping together under one heading a plurality of expressions which derive from the same principle but call for widely different analytical tools and sensibilities. In order to avoid this pitfall, we have limited the present work to two-dimensional works *on paper*.

It may not always be possible to adhere strictly to this plan, for the definition of collage is rather broad, and moreover the painters we will be looking at were constantly taking liberties with the mediums they worked in. But the focus will be on artists who have made a significant use of paper, not only as a support but also as an active element of image making. Their works are comparable to traditional drawings in format as well as in scope; they are also closely related to the written word, the printed page, the formal space of poetry.

From the outset the torn or cut-out pasted paper (and later the Surrealist collage, notably with Max Ernst) functioned in a way that invites comparison with the revolution which poets had conducted in the field of language several decades earlier. The arsenal of avant-garde poetry includes plays on words, on meanings, and even on single letters; typographical experiments; and startling metaphors which combine two elements that appear to have absolutely nothing in common, two radically alien realities, which react with each other and produce a kind of explosion in the reader's imagination. From Mallarmé's *Un Coup de dés* to the chance poems that Tristan Tzara composed by cutting out words and phrases in newspapers, placing them in a hat, and drawing them out at random (not to mention the successive contributions of Apollinaire, Blaise Cendrars, Pierre Reverdy, Max Jacob, and, later, Marinetti and his *parole in libertà*, Hugo Ball, Raoul Hausmann, Kurt Schwitters. the Zaum works of Khlebnikov and Kruchenykh), the fabric of ordinary discourse was shred to pieces. The poets' savage attacks and their subtle irrelevances were designed not only to shake and overturn the old order, but also to regenerate the primitive force of

Olga Rozanova
(1886-1918)
Illustration for *Te li le*, a poem by Alexander Kruchenykh and Velimir Khlebnikov, 1914.

Filippo Tommaso Marinetti
(1876-1944)
Words at Liberty, 1914.
Pen and ink and collage on paper.

words locked—like painting itself—in obsolete descriptive systems.

Finally, let us remember that one of the major literary works of this century was written at the height of the period we are looking at: between 1914 and 1922. The language of James Joyce's *Ulysses*, that enormous and overwhelming novel which abolishes all frontiers, that modernistic poem which combines every genre, from the learned to the grotesque, from alcoholic ravings to the sweet tones of reason, is enriched by foreign or archaic expressions, random quotations, street noises, the ramblings of memory —in other words, all the crude unconscious materials that linger briefly in the modern city dweller's consciousness before sinking back into oblivion.

Jean Huber
(1721-1786)
Lakeside.
Cutout with applied tissue paper.

PRECURSORS ?

MOST books on collage devote a somewhat composite introductory chapter to art works prior to 1912 in which, at one stage or another, the artist used scissors and paste or combined heterogeneous elements. Usually mentioned in this section on the prehistory of collage are twelfth century Japanese calligraphy, fifteenth and sixteenth century Persian bindings, the eighteenth century European art of paper cutouts; as well as religious ex-votos and greeting cards (for New Year's Day, St Valentine's Day, St Catherine's) which perpetuate the memory of ancient magical practices such as summoning a departed relative or reviving a fickle lover's ardour by incorporating different objects or materials pertaining to that person. Traditionally this list also includes folding screens adorned with insipid glued-on images, romantic keepsakes, turn of the century postcards; popular pastimes like silhouette portraits, shadow puppets, childrens' stencils, paper cutouts; not to mention anonymous compositions contrived with butterfly wings, postage stamps, or dry leaves. Rarely, though, do these pleasing, clever, mobile images take us outside the framework of the applied or decorative arts, of family entertainments and quaint dilettantism; and they never call the art of painting into question.

In the field of the fine arts themselves, the first historian of collage, Guillaume Apollinaire, already mentions ancient masters who worked real objects and extraneous materials into their pictures (goldleaf and silverfoil, gems, necklaces, pieces of brocade, inscriptions) in order to increase the sacred character of a holy image. This symbolic realism, which is commonly encountered in Russian icons and in works of the International Gothic style, had its profane equivalent in an altarpiece commissioned by the silk merchants' guild and executed by the Venetian artist Gentile Bellini, who ornamented it with an illusionist landscape entirely composed of multicoloured strips of fabric. Many other examples from remote and less remote ethnic groups could be cited, as could marginal works by isolated artists. Nor would it be difficult to list the various graphic procedures which employ *découpage*, collage, and assemblage (adding readymade faces to portraits and readymade figures to models, inserting side views in perspectives, using superposed plates to teach anatomy, revealing erotic scenes be-

hind "doors and windows" in licentious prints). And yet there is no provable direct link between these works dictated by exceptional circumstances and such products of a fully developed aesthetic as the pasted papers of Braque, Picasso, Schwitters, and Max Ernst.

Perhaps a more fruitful approach would be to examine the works of artists who practised the art of collage without utilizing glue. Adepts of a strictly mental collage, they juxtaposed objects or figures not usually associated in nature or rational thought. The name that springs to mind first is Arcimboldo, perhaps because his genius seems particularly close to the accumulative sensibility of our own period. His *Portraits* and *Seasons* combine independent elements which vehicle both sense and structure. Then there are those geographers of the imagination, the inventors of architectural *Caprices*, like Canaletto and Guardi, who shifted urban monuments as their fancy pleased. One might mention too melancholy dreamers like Grandville, Meryon, Odilon Redon, whose gaze, distended by the fantastic powers of sleep, seems fixed on mirror images of reality, substitutes for reality, realities perpetually seething with sedition. (It was no accident that the Surrealists were to become passionately interested in these artists a few decades later.) Still, there is a real danger in such arbitrary annexations. Far from springing from any radically new insight, the works just mentioned merely exemplify technical devices for creating novel images. Sooner or later, if you succumb to the attractions of the theory of mental collage you wind up viewing all imaginative painting as an aspect of collage, or its product. Actually, collage cannot be reduced to a simple combination of mutually independent elements, however droll or subtle such combinations may seem.

Even a cursory comparison with the odd images called quodlibets (which are sometimes cited as forerunners of collage, doubtless because they use some of the same iconographic motifs: playing cards, pipe tobacco, letters, and newspapers) shows clearly that there is an irreducible difference between modern collage and representations of objects that are governed solely by a desire to counterfeit reality. Using a variety of magical devices, trompe-l'œil attempts to make us believe in a tangible reality which is actually only a use-

less replica, a decoy that fools nobody. Worse, it tries to cover up the tracks of the very act that produces it, as if painting really could fool us by pretending that it is not being taken in by its own deceptions!

Nothing could be further from this art of ideas and technical virtuosity than the forthright honesty of the pasted paper. The sudden energy of collage shatters the fictive pane protecting the image from contingency. Through the shivered glass blows the wind of anarchy. Or rather, by its riotous irruption onto the sheet of paper (clumsily and insolently expressing the promiscuity of things, their "coarse reality," yet at the same time disclosing the gesture which brought them to the surface), the pasted paper heralds the return of the here and now in painting. It proclaims the thusness of Time and Space previously imprisoned (in the trompe-l'œil pictures of John F. Peto or Laurent Dabos for example) in an illusionist allegory designed to isolate them in a glossy, forever unattainable distance. The extraneous fragment reaches out to the viewer's eye. Its just perceptible relief and its different texture and structure tug the eye roughly to the very centre of the work. Modern collage forces us to follow unpredictable, even uninviting byways. It invites us to seek out the hidden side of the decors, the backstage where the enigma of the image is experienced in all its naked intensity. Insofar as it forces our eye to come back to the external world and insofar as it determines how we come to throb in unison with the world, the pasted paper seems to exclude everything prior to its own emergence.

So the question arises whether the real origin of collage is not to be found in a more immediate reality, one that involved artists as early as the beginning of the twentieth century: the reality of the street, of newspapers, of early advertising, of placards posted on city walls, of manufacturers' catalogues. (When Max Ernst leafed through one such catalogue, it suddenly suggested Surrealist collage to him.) The reality the modern urban dweller experienced was a rapidly accelerating one, a reality of widening horizons, of space and time broken up by timetables; of machines, loud noises, news bulletins pouring in from every part of the world; of increasingly frequent and rapid travels. Similarly, the evolution of the new aesthetic should be viewed in relation to the growing importance of photography. Slow steady progress in thought and pictorial technique made painters increasingly aware of instruments that forged their language. It enabled them to discern with increasing clarity the specific properties of those instruments within the context of pictorial syntax. Abandoning to photographers the task of replicating external reality under all its guises (including the picturesque), they began to turn their attention to whatever the camera lens was unable to reproduce: impasto and materials laid on in thick or thin layers, the support's hardness or flexibility, the requirements of format and surface, the transparency or opaqueness of colours, the structure of the composition, the technique of painting (dots or flat tints), the speed of the gestures which spell out the irreplaceable vocabulary of painting, letter by letter.

THE earliest extant examples of pasted papers belong to the art of Japanese calligraphy, whose willowy ideograms inscribe their rhythms on a surface consisting of an assemblage of scraps of wallpaper. From the first, then, we observe a strange complicity between the space of poetry and the materials of interior decoration. It is as if, from the Far Eastern literati down to Guillaume Apollinaire, Braque, and Picasso (not to mention Rilke's admirable *Aufzeichnungen des Malte Laurids Brigge*), the humble yet stubborn patterns of wallpaper are ideally suited to express the mystery that the artist questions. Like a mute, ever available companion, they urge him to continue searching for

the answers. Barely touching the mosaic of various coloured and textured papers ornamented with airy motifs (birds, drifting seeds, languishing blossoms), the painter's vibrant brush sets down the characters of the text he hopes to restore to the soaring freedom of his initial inspiration.

This tradition of picture-poems first appeared in Japan about the twelfth century. It continues to flourish today in the form of birthday greetings exchanged between friends and relatives. Thus, from its very beginning, the technique of the pasted paper associates the imperious presence of an image, whose opaque mass is the first thing the eye encounters, with the endless unfurling of poetic speech that writing precipitates into signs.

Now it is precisely this balance that the European avant-garde artists of the early twentieth century sought to capture and hold in their pasted papers. So the oldest forerunner of collage is perhaps the one that comes closest to its spirit, inasmuch as the act of cutting up or tearing pieces of paper and then assembling them into a new arrangement inspires a meditation on discontinuity (in this case, the passing of the old year, the ineluctable flight of time), while the written poem, that fragile token of eternity, bridges and heals the rift.

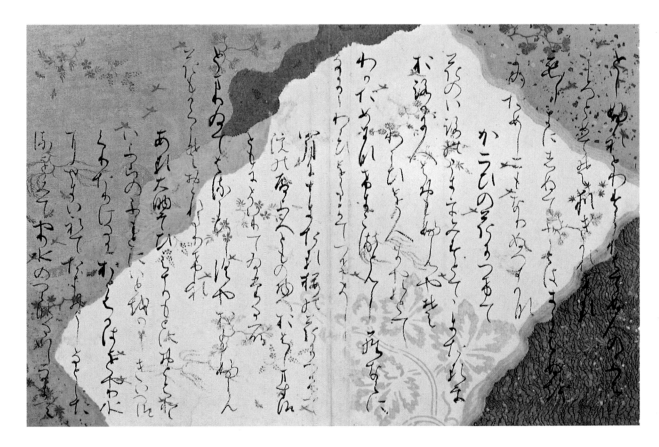

In Europe, the vogue of cut-out papers appears to go back to the sixteenth century when images known as *canivets* were contrived with the aid of a small lancet-like knife that went by the same name. Whole pages of writing and illuminated figures were incised with this instrument, and vellum and parchment were turned into lace. Initially limited to holy images ornamenting passionals, psalmbooks, and books of hours, this highly dexterous work spread to decorating workshops where it was applied to folding screens, fire-screens, book bindings, and boxes and chests of every description. In the eighteenth century, the vogue reached such proportions that "everyone, from the highest to the lowest" practised the art of cutouts. A flourishing industry of pre-cut ornaments and ready-to-cut patterns popularized a rather trite repertoire of images which included small, generally entertaining rustic scenes that repeated the same motifs *ad nauseam* (flowers, butterflies and other insects), hunting scenes, lovers' trysts, ornamental flower arrangements, shepherdesses surrounded by sheep. Chinoiseries, pirouetting exotic animals, and somersaulting acrobats described often vertiginous arabesques that lent themselves admirably to the lancet's curving strokes.

"Canivet"
(France, 18th century)
Paper cutout heightened with grey wash.

▷ **Jean Huber**
(1721-1786)
Gymnasium.
Paper cutout with pencil strokes.

TOWARDS the middle of the eighteenth century this fashion was succeeded by a fad for cut-out portraits, ironically named "silhouette portraits" after the French finance minister Etienne de Silhouette who recommended them as an inexpensive substitute for painting. Economical indeed, they reduce the human face to a severe profile yet ensure a likeness that satisfied both the fond gaze of lovers and the scientist's scrutiny of the physiognomist Johann Caspar Lavater. The work of the Geneva artist Jean Huber has a place of its own, one that deserves wider recognition, among the products of this enormously popular art that is still practised today in remote rural districts. Although his small silhouette sketches of Voltaire earned him a certain notoriety in his lifetime (their sharp outlines mock the somethat breathless nimble-ness of the old man of Ferney), his large "cut-out pictures," as he called them, were unknown except to a small circle of connoisseurs which included Baron Grimm, their most ardent admirer. Huber's subjects were borrowed from the monumental painting of his day—hunting scenes, landscapes, antique ruins. His compositions were exceptionally large; and he created an astonishing variety of effects with the scalpel, ranging from minute touches to bold, sweeping strokes. This enabled him to shape wonderfully expressive spaces and to invent an undeniably original plastic language. He himself was aware of this, as his letters show: "My pictures should be viewed as a kind of Sculpture. They are Pictures that invite Thought. They persuade the Spectator's Imagination to obey the bidding of simple Contours."

IF TO paste is to add and to cut out is to remove, then the combination of these acts can only result in an image with a double meaning, or rather an image with a visual double entendre. This is the case with works that conceal part of their meaning either to ridicule a hypocrisy or to screen an arcane message from the ordinary viewer. It is also the case with anatomical or architectural plates which use transparency to build up a meaning in several layers. They combine the outer shell and the inner structure, the envelope and the organs, on the same plane and in the same temporal frame. A detail of clothing, furniture, or anatomy serves as a flap which can either conceal or reveal a humorous or scandalous truth that qualifies the image's literal meaning. An antipapist print of the sixteenth century, for example, secretes a variety of misdeeds behind the sovereign pontiff's ample vestment:

lift up the little tab pasted to the image and you uncover wars, heretics being burned at the stake, scenes of extortion and simony.

In the same vein, the prints known as "Doors and Windows" (*Portes et Fenêtres*) enjoyed an extraordinary vogue in the nineteenth century. Artists like Monnier, Devéria, and Traviès were unashamed to use their gifts on these naive riddles. To be sure, these seemingly harmless images were far from being as innocent as they appeared: they were a way of circumventing the censor's office as well as titillating the viewer. In the "adult" picture shown here the lithographer's name and the publishers' address have been omitted, and the expected image has been replaced by an erotic scene. The anonymous artist has reinforced the effect of joyous surprise by creating a parallel between two unpredictably incongruous realities.

Un billet, Monsieur, pour qui me prenez-vous!

Anonymous
(19th century)
"A ticket, sir? What do you take me for?"
Plates from *Les portes et fenêtres*, Paris, c. 1835.
Coloured lithographs.

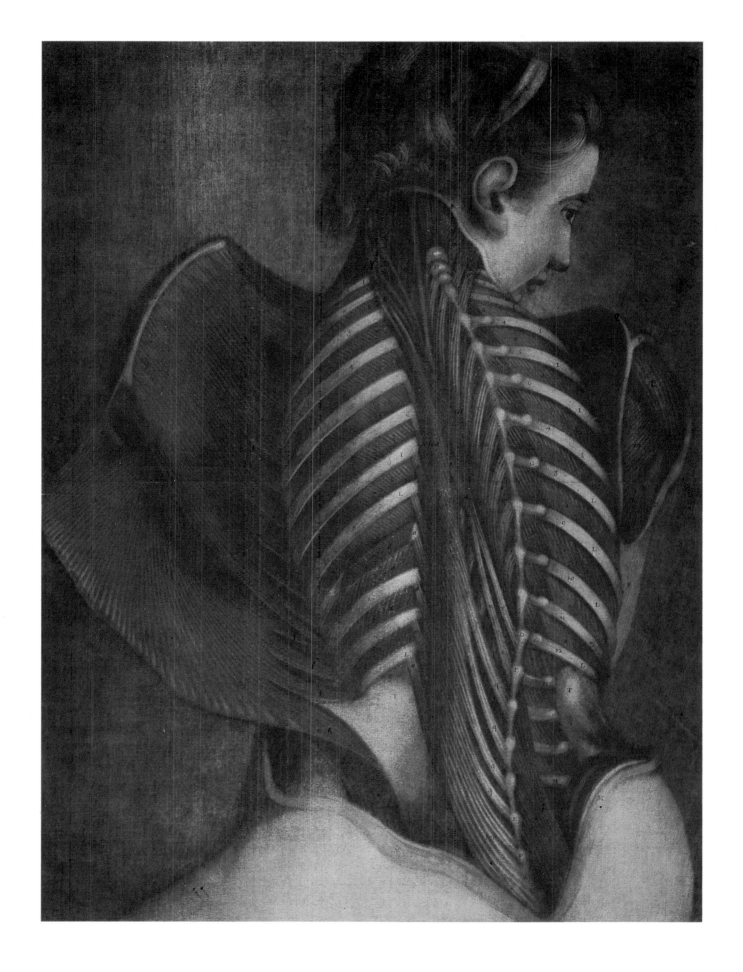

Jacques Gautier d'Agoty
(1710-1781)
The Anatomical Angel.
Coloured aquatint.

J.S. Paan
(later 18th century)
Trompe l'oeil collage, Holland, 1779.
Watercolour, pen and ink, collage.

Johann Jakob Hauswirth
(1808-1871)
Paper Cutout, 1859.

APART from his writing, Victor Hugo was intensely active as a draughtsman. As an artist he was able to express his eye's extraordinary appetite for the whole universe, from its most enduring forms down to its smallest, most fleeting details. His visionary genius was forever alert to the endless possibilities teeming in ink washes. He was fascinated by transformations of meaning obtained with stencils or by folding, using fabrics of different textures and paper of different thicknesses, superposing writing and images. Thus Hugo seems to have anticipated the displaced sensibility that was to lead the artists of the early 1900s to examine the mechanics of image making. His abundant experiments with combining techniques, his efforts to wring new visual statements from resistant materials, his fondness for startling juxtapositions, and his willingness to capitalize on any opportunity offered by random combinations announce the spirit of contemporary collage. Yet the visiting card shown here, addressed to friends early in 1855 from the poet's remote exile on the island of Jersey, can be seen as a return to the propitiatory practices of the most primitive examples of collage—the religious ex-votos or animistic totems, the images used to cast a spell, the birthday greetings, the valentines—that strive to abolish distance and the pain of absence by inserting a personal item.

Victor Hugo
(1802-1885)
Visiting Card, 1855.
Pen and ink, gouache, collage.

Pablo Picasso
(1881-1973)

Glass and Bottle of Suze, autumn 1912.
Pasted paper, gouache, charcoal.

A NEW MACHINE FOR SEEING

THE sight of a roll of wallpaper in an Avignon shop-window, in late August 1912, gave Georges Braque the revelation of the pasted paper and the possibilities offered by this technique. Was the artist fully aware of the consequences this discovery was to have on the future of perception? Although he communicated nearly all of his aesthetic preoccupations to Picasso that summer, Braque kept the discovery to himself for several days. Perhaps he sensed that his sudden intuition, which enthralled yet alarmed him, would open a breach through which the whole of modernity in painting was to flood? What is certain, at all events, is that as soon as he returned to Sorgues in September 1912, Braque began to work with strips of industrially prepared paper, shaping it roughly with scissors, positioning it with his fingers, and then pasting it to a support. Viewed in the context of Braque's and Picasso's joint experiments with space and pictorial reality, this development seems, if not inevitable, at least a logical outcome of their investigations. It is also a decisive turning point in the history of Western art, and indeed of Western thought.

Since 1908, Picasso and Braque had been absorbed in a joint exploration that supposed a degree of reciprocal trust and friendship rarely encountered in the arts. Inspired by Cézanne's example as well as by black African art (with its realism which is the reverse of Western realism, though it is just as potent) they struggled jointly to replace the perspectivist mode founded on Alberti's idealist theories with a new optical order that would be both closer to the data of experience and the sense perceptions and truer to the specific nature of painting.

Actually, at the point when the two artists began their joint undertaking the long-standing Illusionism of Western art was already coming under attack. A large number of painters were rallying to the idea that the real issue of painting lay within the exciting, strictly delimited area enclosed by the picture frame. Some of them were using thick impasto to stress the physical presence of pigment. Others were employing unmixed colours, strong contours that isolated forms, divisionist brushstrokes. Still others were allowing increasingly visible blank spaces to appear on the canvas; they were emphasizing the texture of the support and, increasingly, leaving the image unfinished.

Simultaneously, the subject and all that it implied (the outward wealth of painting) was gradually losing its clarity of outline. Its pre-eminent status was being undermined, in some cases wholly destroyed, by an increasing attention to the interplay of forms. It was as if the new painters, in their haste to invent a new vocabulary, were relegating the subject to a subaltern position, turning it into a mere pretext. Obviously something in the admirable independent order that had kept the world spellbound with illusions was collapsing. With the advent of Cubism a flood of disconnected pictorial forms was released. Reading a painting was no longer a simple affair; it was no longer possible to glide effortlessly to the point where one feels one has grasped a picture. It was as if, to paraphrase Andersen's fairy tale of the emperor's new clothes, a voice had suddenly begun to shout insolently: "The picture isn't a window on the world!" This gave a new slant to the viewer's reading of the painting and forced his gaze to turn back from the illusionist depth to the picture plane.

As early as Picasso's *Demoiselles d'Avignon*, painted in the winter of 1906-1907, pictorial space was compressed by a violence and fragmentariness that thrust it towards the surface. The spectator's eye was made to grope painfully through a universe in shambles. Planes overlapped, angles jutted out unexpectedly. Under the pressure of forces that unfolded them and revealed them as a jumble of facet-planes, objects were brutally flattened so that they coincided with the picture plane. Instead of receding along perspective lines that converge on a single point, the forms in the composition projected outwards as if they were reaching towards the viewer. An urgent expressive need propelled them towards the eye, forcing the beholder to notice their texture, their naked material beauty.

This is probably the reason why the Cubist painters soon gave up doing portraits and landscapes (a genre that is narrowly tied to depth) and concentrated instead on rendering familiar objects that fit into the hand—newspapers, glasses, packs of tobacco—or that spring to life the moment they are touched—mandolins and guitars, playing cards, dice, pipes. Thus they gradually established an anti-illusionist space, or rather a space stripped of illusions. They broke up the reality of ephemeral appearances that are forever eluding our grasp. In their disintegrated reality the mind is penetrated by the essence of things. In their seething space everything (volumes, colours, forms, the space between objects, lighting) is subordinated to the artist's desire to produce an image that answers both to the truth of the object being represented and to the requirements of the pictorial surface which he is now committed to respect.

Inspired by this twofold ideal and determined to make their patient mental reconstructions of reality universally legible, Braque and Picasso each in turn introduced into his pictures elements that were recognizable to the eye yet totally alien to the rigorous spatial definition of early Cubism. Take the famous trompe-l'œil nail with its cast shadow, a novel paradox in painting. Does it signal a return to reality or is it simply a device for reminding us of the artist's omnipotence? Does it indicate depth or is it on the contrary an affirmation of the picture plane? Or consider the stencilled numbers and letters which inscribe an apparent neutrality at the heart of the work yet also suggest, by force of contrast, that the bodies in the pictorial space are both mobile and transparent. Consider the keys sticking out of locks, the drawer pulls, the fragmentary newspaper banners: tokens of a sensibility that has opened to the world, they baffle the viewer, through metonymic allusions to complex bodies, with a thickening flurry of changing rhythms and planes. Finally, consider the "old-fashioned procedures" that Picasso mentions in a letter to Braque dated 7 October 1912: imitations of marble or wood-grain, preparations made with sand that "glue" our eye to the picture plane and compensate for the extreme fragmentation of forms and the restricted colour range.

◁ **Georges Braque**
(1882-1963)
Pipe, Glass and Die, 1914.
Charcoal and pasted paper.

Juan Gris
(1887-1927)
The Book, February 1913.
Oil and pasted paper on canvas.

Now this complex rhetoric consisting of endless permutations and elisions is wholly contained in the pasted paper. It sustains it, it calls it into existence. The day Braque's restless intellect suddenly grasped the new technique's potential, he set in motion both a visual mechanics (a "new machine for seeing," as its most discerning student, Jean Paulhan, was to call it) and an actual Copernican revolution in painting. Yet several decades were to pass before the full significance of this revolution became clear. The pasted paper did not burst into the sacred grove of painting all at once: it crept into it stealthily, with a gentle impertinence. True, the Cubist painters shattered the convention of meticulous craftsmanship, the tradition of noble materials inspired with a noble intention, and they chose instead to imitate the house painter's example, the "fast gesture" (to cite Isabelle Monod-Fontaine's felicitous term). They even claimed to scorn the artist's personality and they proclaimed a natural inclination for poverty and the unfinished. Yet the facetious spirit which they brought to their work seems almost intimidated by its own daring. The Cubists' cautious restraint is particularly surprising when you consider the loud public declarations and violent anathematizing of other contemporary avant-garde movements.

Mainly, though, it is a return to reality in painting that is being affirmed by the arbitrary forms cut out of rolls of wallpaper imitating wood panelling, veined marble, or floral motifs; the scraps torn from newspapers with their fragmentary news; the apéritif labels and cigarette packs that Braque, Picasso, and, later, Juan Gris were including in their pictures. It is an immediate, banal or ironic, often incomplete reality. Though it is devoid of charm and of any aesthetic intention, it nevertheless vehicles a rough-and-ready yet extraordinarily fragile assurance.

The soiled, worn state of the elements taken from manufactured items, and the almost anonymous process by which they were assembled, express an experience of poverty and privation, a universe whose horizons (formerly the theatre of dreams) have contracted to a studio's walls, to the sides of a table laden with a few personal belongings or common musical instruments. Jettisoning the varnishes, scumbles, and hazy finishes of academic painting, turning their backs on the cold prospects, the unattainable distances of classical landscapes, the Cubist painters thrust us into the noisy, disorderly intimacy of ordinary objects shared over a glass of wine in the warm haze of cigarette smoke and talk. This unmediated communion with the mysterious beauty of common matter is, more

Pablo Picasso
(1881-1973)
Guitar, spring 1913.
Pasted paper.

than anything else, what gives the pasted paper its virile straightforwardness.

Yet once the initial moment of surprise—and pleasure—has passed, our perception of the pictorial space is undermined by a series of extremely bewildering effects produced by the collaged elements. The physical position of the different scraps of paper, the subtle overlappings, the differences of colour and texture that make each fragment stand out from its neighbours as well as from the surface onto which it is glued, the interaction of the collaged elements and pencil lines: all of this produces a shuttling movement which causes each plane to contrast or break with its neighbours and to stand out in its turn on the picture surface. Far from being apprehended in a coherent well-rehearsed cognitive process, the pictorial depth is deduced from elements that crowd towards the surface. In some cases they even extrude from the surface into actual space, as if they were impatient to escape from the traditional restraints of painting. This is true of the constructions made of folded strips of paper, the guitars made of assembled planes, that Picasso (and Braque too, though none of the latter's pictorial "sculptures" have been preserved) pressed into

three-dimensional space. All of the pasted papers dating from this period (especially those Picasso, with supreme nonchalance, simply pinned to the support) produce this indeterminate spatial effect and suggest—yet simultaneously withhold from our perception—an extra spatial dimension.

The Cubist artists soon added other rifts to this initial rupture in pictorial continuity. Taking one side of a cut-out fragment they would make it overlap on a neighbouring form, which would then in turn overlap on the initial fragment (see Picasso's *Still Life with Pipe* on page 39). Or—and this was the case with almost all of Braque's pasted papers—an object's contour would be drawn with apparent clumsiness over the material intended to describe it. Sometimes colours would be allowed to spill over forms that were meant to contain them; at other times lines would stray freely from the colours they were supposed to delimit. These perversions of the optical process by which we apprehend planes, these non-congruent colours and forms, give us the feeling that objects have a certain transparency relative to one another, that they are indeed essentially transparent. In a space convulsed with inner movement, an arena of visual

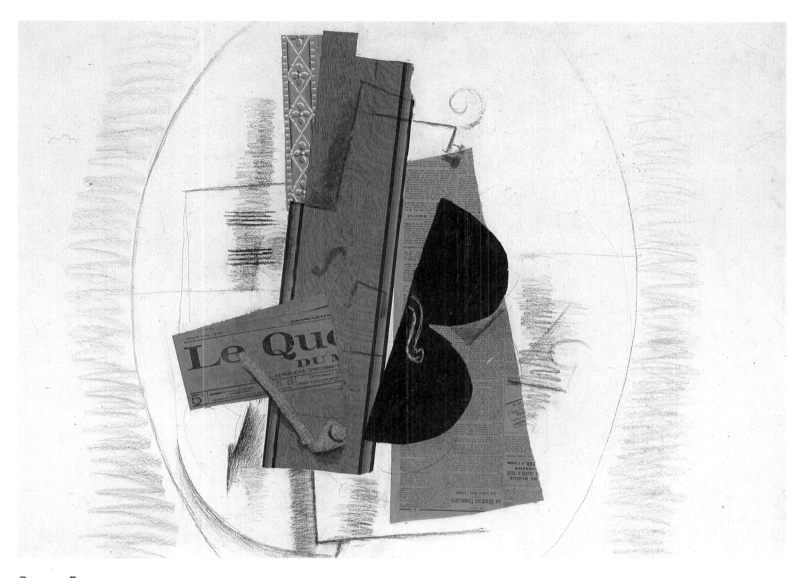

Georges Braque
(1882-1963)
Violin and Pipe, 1913-1914.
Charcoal and pasted paper on cardboard.

transformations, substitutions, and overlappings as frequent as they are shortlived, bodies inevitably lose their opaqueness. Subjected one and all to the same savage two-dimensionality, they are open to every possible kind of reciprocal penetration and simultaneity. In this sense, it is fair to state that the Cubist concept increases the angles from which things are viewed, not with the intention of viewing them from all sides, as has often been claimed, but so as to induce them to disclose their essence, the unique coherence expressed in their different facets.

This cunning interplay of visual combinations (complicated at times by their inventors' fondness for the ambiguities of classical trompe-l'œil with its false wood-grains, its imitation mouldings, its cast shadows) tends in the end to make us aware of the incalculable number of contradictory relationships which interact with our retina, the reality of the outer world, and the specific field of painting. When we enter the space of a pasted paper image and submit to its active disorder—when we surrender to its powers of persuasion—we find ourselves obliged to interpret the signs which materialize the image. Our eye cannot dissociate the pleasure of contemplating the image

from the material, tactile presence of the elements that make up the surface of the picture.

The invention of the Cubist *papier collé* contains a parable that sheds light on the whole field of modern painting. This is the declaration that the faculty of sight is no longer adequate to apprehend the new reality of space; that, faced with the disappearance of the familiar conventions and reference points that sustained the pictorial illusion in the past, modern man is obliged to call on new perceptual resources. As with the tale of the apostle who remains incredulous despite the evidence of his own eyes, the pasted paper picture invites us to reach out and feel its surface with our fingers. The pasted paper revolution compensated, with remarkable speed and lack of regrets, for the failure of an entire system by asserting the physical reality of matter. What we experience before these works of a moving simplicity is a total involvement of the senses, akin to that which we feel on hearing a cello's gruff tones blending, under the musician's attack, the shuddering of wooden components—pegs, sound-post, and bridge—with the instrument's surge into effortlessness, the moan of the strings, and the invisible sounds escaping therefrom.

HERE are some of the very earliest experiments with pasted papers. Braque has been using this technique for several days, perhaps several weeks, and yet how masterfully and powerfully he employs it! In art—as can never be repeated often enough—the first fruits of a technical innovation almost always coincide with fully mature aesthetic effects. The artist's eye and hand, in joint eagerness to discover the secret that they sense within reach, combine proficiency and daring to create works of an accuracy and freshness that will never be repeated, at least not in the same proportions and not with the same felicity and acuity. Before this starkly simple and mysterious work, which Georges Braque composed in the summer of 1912, we experience something of the astonishment that its first viewers doubtless felt. Aside from the shock value, then, of intruding a foreign substance into a painting and abandoning the artist's traditionally recognized privilege of exercising his mastery to create an illusory reality, the overwhelming anonymous mass of colour that invades the white page here (permeating it and at the same time appearing to push out from the surface) is deeply troubling to the eye. In the almost total absence of figurative reference that characterizes this phase of Cubist analysis, in the subtle and fragmentary evocation of an object summarized with a handful of lines, an object reduced so to speak to colourlessness and nuancelessness, the large swatch of paper suddenly acquires, with no apparent artistic expertness, no sensual forms or colours, a decisive pneumatic force of its own. It gives life and weight to the composition. The mere presence of the found material makes the composition immediately credible to the senses. The tangibility of the collaged matter compensates for the indefiniteness of a visible order on the brink of extinction.

The importance given to the sense of touch (the thickness of the scrap of paper pasted to the support produces a very slight relief that is nevertheless sufficient to anchor the fragment in actual space) is undercut by various semantic analogies and spatial transformations. Almost at once the eye reasserts itself, warning us that the fragment from which we have just derived such a keen sense of reality is in fact nothing more than a deception, a vulgar imitation, a scrap of fake wood-grain. Yet no sooner do we pause to examine this first disarming paradox than our mind (by a process which is familiar, even if the name is not —synecdoche) promptly associates the trompe-l'œil substance with the object identified by signs scattered through the composition: the sound-holes, pegs, scroll-like curves, and strings that designate a violin. The artist's use of the pasted paper is thus neither as innocent nor quite as arbitrary as it first seemed. Though it is intended to describe an actual property of the object being represented (in this case, the material it is made from) the pasted paper does not function in a way that satisfies natural logic. Quite the contrary, just as the Cubist analysis of forms breaks up the object's unity and attempts to render its many facets in space rather than to recompose its visual appearance, so the strip of coloured material does not strictly fit the violin, but suggests it rather. It does not seek to imitate, and it does not promise any full conjunction. This fragmentary, chaotic reading of the image produces, as if by contagion, further permutations which interfere with, yet enrich, the act of seeing. Consider the optical exchange between the charcoal lines of the drawing and the pasted paper: just where do we situate the latter? To the front or to the rear of the composition? Part of the violin (the pegs and the neck, the curves of the body and the bridge) is drawn directly on the pasted paper, so that the latter appears to sink into depth. Yet the pasted paper's tangible character, its pictorial value—imitating the instrument's wood-grain—and, mainly, the opening of the actually cut out sound-hole, propel it towards the surface.

Finally, what are we to make of the three letters BAL? How can they possibly be inscribed across both the pasted paper and the blank support? A considerable mental effort is required to establish this word's semantic and spatial relevance, for it seems to have no connection at all to the visual description. The answer to this riddle, the last of several posed by the artist, is not contained in the image's syntax but revolves around an optical memory of transparency. Reading the work backwards, as it were, our mind and sense perceptions jointly reconstruct the original situation: a violin resting on a (wooden?) table seen through the plate glass window of a café advertising dancing (BAL).

The point, however, is not that a given situation has been evoked (for it was also revoked the moment it became the subject of a painting) but that we have been led, by a process that is in many respects a magical one, from a simple vision of depth rendered two-dimensionally to a powerful experience of penetrating into a space whose signs, crowding upwards and deploying on the picture plane, invite us to perceive an extra dimension.

Georges Braque
(1882-1963)
Violin Still Life with BAL, 1912.
Charcoal and pasted paper.

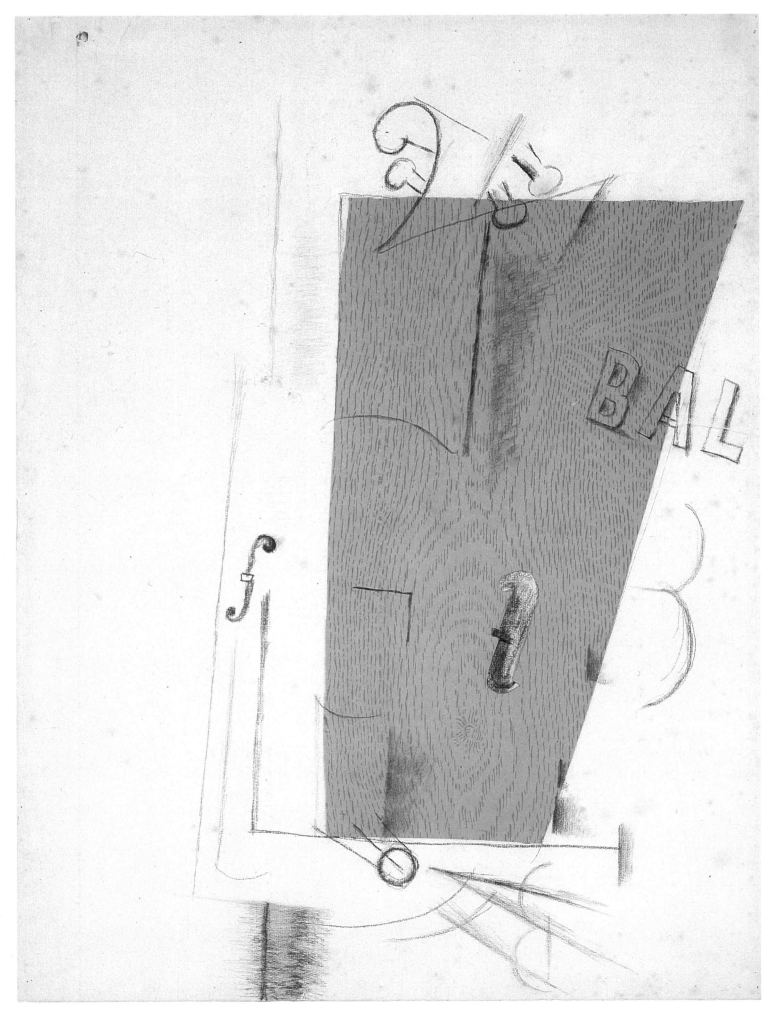

STRICTLY speaking, the idea of collage seems to have come from Picasso who, as early as May 1912, introduced a swatch of oilcloth imitating a chair's cane-bottom into an oval still life (page 10) framed by a length of thick rope. With this doubly iconoclastic gesture he banished the precious materials, exclusiveness, and sham prestige of easel painting and replaced them with the informal manner of an artist who saw himself as a sort of mechanic labouring to bring about a new way of seeing. So it was with a particularly sharp interest that Picasso examined the first pasted paper experiments Braque showed him after his return to Paris. After a pause for reflection, Picasso appropriated this "paperistic technique" (as he called it) with the passionate inventiveness and restless curiosity that he displays at each major turn of his career. It promptly became his favourite means for carrying out the experiments he was conducting at the time to determine the basic elements of pictorial syntax.

Between October 1912 and March 1913 Picasso produced more than one hundred collages. And while Braque in the meantime was following up his own initial intuitions, working at his own pace towards superbly balanced large compositions like *Aria de Bach* and *Glass, Clarinet and Newspaper*, the Spanish artist, for his part, was experimenting in all directions. He began by extending the repertoire of found manufactured items: geometric and floral wallpapers, wrapping paper of different hues, music paper, visiting cards, bottle labels, tobacco packs, match books, and of course newspaper clippings (which he employed at times mainly for their formal value, at other times mainly as realist indications, but almost always playing on both aspects at once). Next he increased the number of permutations between the different collaged substances; and then between the collaged substance itself and the armature of drawn lines that holds it in place. In variation after variation, he reversed relationships and modulated accents, as if to verify the efficacy of his discoveries at each successive stage. Finally, as new solutions were suggested by these permutations of found papers, he would try them out in painting and sculpture (they were in turn enriched and transfigured by this exchange). Picasso's openness to tangible materials and his delight in their transformations and revelations undoubtedly springs from his fastidious, systematic examination of the technical innovations that were revolutionizing traditional art: the pasted paper (whether cut-out, glued, or pinned to the support), pigment mixed with sand, industrial paints, assemblage, *pliage*, and the practice of including and combining all sorts of real objects on the canvas.

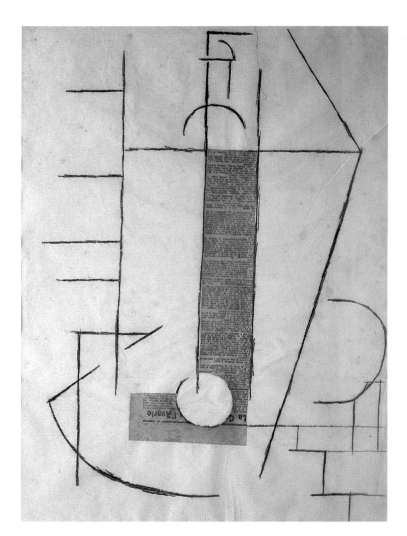

Pablo Picasso
(1881-1973)
Bottle on a Table, autumn-winter 1912.
Charcoal and pasted paper.

This inventiveness which reflected on its own daring as it continued to stride forwards allowed the artist to acquire gradually an intellectual mastery of the foundations of visual language. By enabling him to gauge and compare minutely calculated effects, a series of pasted papers executed towards the end of 1912 prepared the ground for painting's complete emancipation from the model. In a picture like *Bottle on a Table*, the spare armature of pencil lines, to which a strip of cut-out newspaper is added, is in fact a condemnation of the subjection of tangible reality to the idiom of strong simple signs that was then being developed in Cubist painting. Yet, despite the extreme graphic reduction of the objects in the collage, the work remains legible thanks to the mental process which enables us to reconstruct a coherent whole from gaping lacunae (though it is a coherence that is forever eluding us). It is as if we were able, by virtue of some fragile, unspectacular mechanism, to enter into the very process of seeing. It is as if we were able to go a step beyond synthesis and participate in the reversals, the ellipses, the substitutions, the simultaneity, the lapses, the returns that from second to second mark the internal labour of the eye.

THE splendid *Still Life with Pipe* of 1913-1914 is a moving testimonial to this sudden acceleration of the visual process. An oval, cut out roughly from a sheet of wrapping paper, condenses the ideated space described by means of scanty almost ironically scrupulous pencil lines: a room, a table top, and a few ordinary objects scattered about (a glass, a pipe, a pack of pipe tobacco). These objects are really only pretexts which the artist, using cutouts, summarizes into concepts rather than link them to outer appearances. Colour is completely dissociated from the support with which it would coincide in an ordinary view. Instead it is suggested by a strip of wallpaper placed vertically across the composition with a complete indifference to plausibility.

The paste and the casually placed pins that unite the collage's disparate elements are not governed by an organic principle that safeguards the equilibrium of the image threatened with being torn apart. Does this work in fact still pertain to the art of drawing? Doesn't it answer instead to other requirements, requirements that are no longer altogether those of painting and not yet wholly those of sculpture? Our eye hesitates and is baffled by this seething surface which appears to push back the frame's limits. In the absence of any trace of perspective or shading, the space defined by the association of isolated fragments begins to revolve, to scatter the bodies which inhabit it; it stretches their volumes, dissociates their properties, reveals their hidden angles. The image's material signs, thrust upwards by this spatial insurrection, give our eye no alternative but to recognize the peremptory reality of painting and its ingredients. Yet they also confuse us with a bewildering array of contradictory planes, transformations, and interruptions which succeed one another at a dizzy pace. With a kind of precipitate honesty, the Cubist collage declares the immediacy of things, their propinquity. It enables us to touch the reassuring husk of tangible reality, and then the very precariousness of its assemblage immediately destroys this assurance. It is thanks to this that we are able to deduce depth. As if we were waking from a

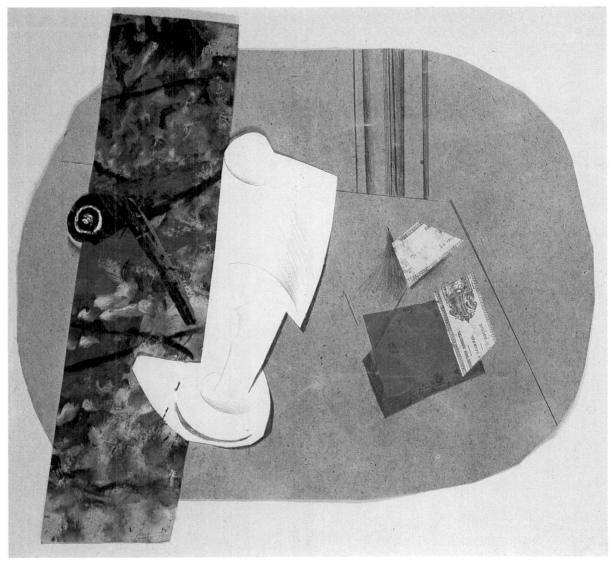

Pablo Picasso
(1881-1973)
Still Life with Pipe, 1913-1914.
Pinned and pasted paper and pencil.

brief nap, before our consciousness is fully able to re-establish the meaning of things, we experience in front of this image and others like it the simultaneous jarring of a multitude of visual entities converging indiscriminately on our retina in a space from which all familiar bearings have been removed. Tangible yet transparent, hollow yet crowded, it is actually a sort of non-space that memory and our experience of the real world nevertheless succeed in recomposing a second later. The effect of surprise and disruption that Picasso's pasted paper produces is of the same order as the bafflement we feel when we first perceive things in the self-declaring nakedness and radiant isolation of their emergence. In the instant before our mind performs the act of synthesis that allows it to regain its briefly threatened poise, we glimpse them on the "threshold of transparency."

At the very moment, then, that he was devising new weapons (testing their sharpness in scores of experiments between 1912 and 1914) the artist was, perhaps defiantly, compressing the arena where the eye's struggle takes place. Remembering the space where the matador's bright figure was pitted against the bull's dark power, only millimetres away, Picasso endeavoured to place his creative gestures on the thin dividing line between a threatening multitudinous exterior and the imperatives of the work: that hair's-breadth fissure where the outer world, suddenly called into question, surrenders its space to art's space.

Series of pasted papers on the wall of Picasso's studio, 242 Boulevard Raspail, Paris, 1912.
Photograph.

Juan Gris
(1887-1927)
Violin and Hanging Print, April 1913.
Oil, sand and collage on canvas.

HAVING joined Cubism towards 1911, Juan Gris soon assimilated its basic tenets. Unlike Picasso and Braque, who were still cautiously testing their innovations and discoveries, Gris elaborated deeply thought out pictures from the principles he deduced from their work. Gris' contribution to Cubism (that intellectual enterprise characterized by a passionate involvement with objects and a quest for language that would describe them more searchingly) was at once an uncompromising approach to method and a solid respect for the specific means of painting. Gris cared too much about the tangible presence of things to relinquish all exterior effects—especially effects of lighting—which give body to volumes and colours. (In this, he was again unlike Picasso and Braque who were ready to sacrifice everything in their ruthless questioning of

reality and their search for its essence.) Gris never reduced shapes to the bare, abstract forms you find in some of Picasso's contemporary pasted paper compositions. Though he began by subordinating images to the imperatives of a sovereign intellectual architecture, he never failed, once these were satisfied, to nuance his compositions with feeling. Sober and silent, his work (a classical oeuvre if there ever was one) seesaws between the Spartan virtues of definition and the appeal of evocation.

In fact, there is something symbolic about the way Juan Gris included pasted items in his pictures. (He adopted this technique in the autumn of 1912.) Instead of using collage to disrupt space, he applied it in a traditional way (at least in his early experiments), in order to strengthen the reality of his images. In the

41

Book (February 1913) two pages scissored from a novel occupy the ''real'' space created by previously fragmented forms. To satisfy the same requirements of illusionist realism, the artist inserted a piece of mirror in the *Washbasin* (1912) : obviously the mirror's glitter could not have been rendered as sharply by pictorial means alone. In none of these examples does collage produce the spatial breaks and semantic inversions one usually encounters in early Cubist pasted papers. Gris' extraneous materials have a kind of staidness, not unlike the dispassionate composure of Duchamp's Readymades but without their irony. This is exemplified in a letter Gris wrote to his friend and dealer D.H. Kahnweiler in September 1913. Referring to *Violin and Hanging Print*, Gris remarked: ''Since Monsieur Brenner owns the picture, he is perfectly entitled to substitute something else for the print— even his own portrait, if he wishes. The result may or may not be an improvement, as when you frame a picture, but the actual nature of the picture can't be altered.''

BUT then, in 1914, a change took place. Gris, having absorbed the intricate principle of the pasted paper in Braque's and Picasso's works, now began to include large pieces of paper cut into simple, effective shapes. He relied on these shapes to organize a spatial matrix over which he then added his deft brushstrokes. Though not allowing the pasted fragment complete autonomy, though touching up colours and textures (imitating wood grain and veined marble) or masking breaks under gouache or cast shadows drawn with a pencil, he yielded none the less to the attractions of collage's inexhaustible combinations. He could not help it that the extraneous materials he selected influenced the carefully worked out organization of the picture surface (to which, in his view of pictorial synthesis, each item in the picture must be subordinated). Nor could he prevent imbricating planes, overlapping textures and colours, from opening up the picture surface and making it lighter and airier. Every one of the sophisticated works he composed in 1914, especially the large *Fruitdish and Carafe*, evokes objects seen through a prism—broken up, multiplied, displaced items whose different angles and facets we view in succession. On the one hand, each glued fragment seems to ''detach'' a pictorial sign from its representational foundation and give it independence; on the other, it links the sign referentially to our grasp of the object. Swept up in a movement that leads from the necessary to the arbitrary, the eye alternately fastens on familiar shapes and surrenders to the vertigo of abstraction. Contemplating the characteristic checkerboard pattern of the Cubist works of this period, it shifts from square to square, seeking more abstruse, unpredictable and frail optical combinations.

Juan Gris
(1887-1927)
Study of a Violin, 1916.
Pencil.

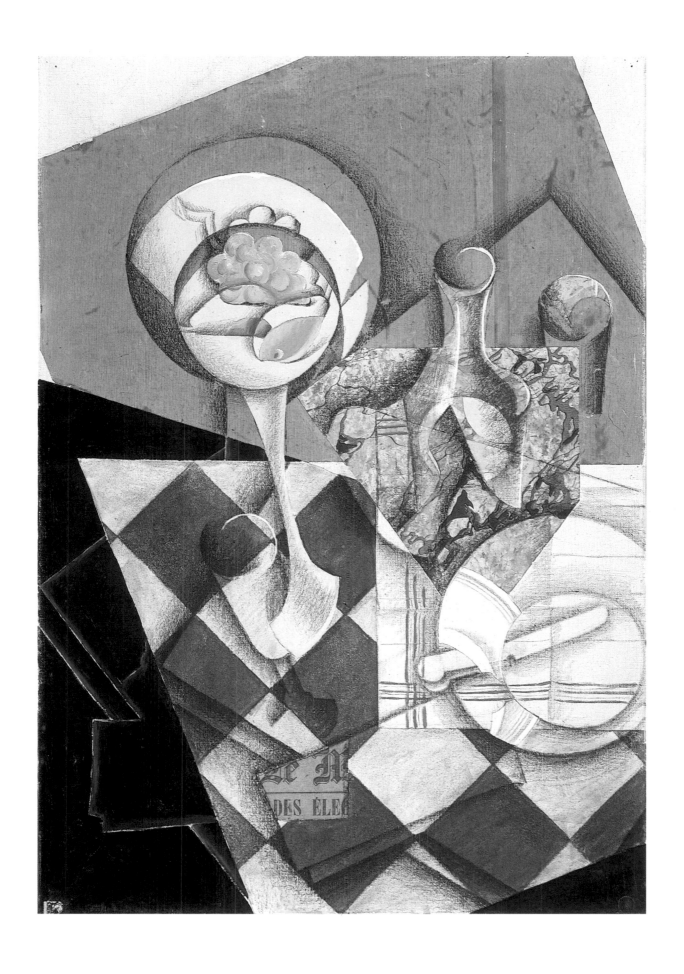

Juan Gris
(1887-1927)
Fruitdish and Carafe, 1914.
Oil, charcoal and pasted paper on canvas.

PICASSO'S cardboard and sheet metal constructions show, from 1912 on, how readily the pasted paper calls forth three-dimensional space. With these arrangements of overlapping cut-out planes, crisp edges which produce a slight relief, and palpably different textures, we are already well on the way to sculpture. So it seems natural that, in 1915, Henri Laurens, encouraged by his friend Braque and by Picasso's guitars, began to adapt the principle of two-dimensional assemblage to constructions in space: in a sense, his hand and eye were already at home in collage. With Laurens, the pasted paper and the three-dimensional construction have the same origin; they stem from the same meditation about the art of sculpture. And, in fact, for several years Laurens experimented simultaneously with sculpture and collage. The result was that his sculpture soon underwent a radical change: it lost its ample volumes and became characterized by arrangements of thin planes that break up light into coloured surfaces. These fragment the unity of the masses arrayed around a single axis, separated by openings and passages replete with vacant space (and consequently as present, as totally *there*, as solid forms). Bronze and stone, which had supplied the weight that kept Laurens' figures anchored to the floor, were replaced by lightweight materials (wood, cardboard, aluminium foil, cloth, small found objects) which impart a different sort of gravity to his sculptures. His three-dimensional works no longer rested on sturdy bases, but were now light enough to be supported by a shelf or table, a nail in the wall, if not thin air.

In his first pasted papers, using precise geometrical shapes—triangles, circles, rectangles—scissored from sheets of (for the period) unusually sober paper, Laurens showed a propensity for the attractions of equilibrium (or rather the perils of disequilibrium). With a series of clowns, jugglers, and dancers—including *Josephine Baker* (1915), with her limbs stretched at almost impossible angles—he sought to express the restless relationship between form and space, the threat of disintegration contained in a construction's very nucleus. There is something of the tightrope walker about Laurens, an amateurish, mocking clownishness. His work has a gimcrack quality, but there seems to be no limit to its tenderness or to the seriousness with which he approaches his materials and art.

Henri Laurens
(1885-1954)
Josephine Baker, 1915.
Pasted paper, pencil, white crayon, gouache.

In the many still life collages which Gris composed from 1916 on, the contours of cut-out objects unfold space three-dimensionally. Their imbricated shapes, their contrasts, their negative forms and spaces, their chromatic repetitions and echoes—over which the artist adds brief pencilled notations which suggest added transparent layers—invite us to slip behind the object, to circle around it (e.g. this *Bottle and Newspaper*). Thanks to this stratagem, the actual movement that underlies our reading of a three-dimensional work, determining the space in which we move about as we view it, is projected onto the support.

Henri Laurens
(1885-1954)
Woman with Mantilla, 1916.
Pasted paper.

Bottle and Newspaper, 1916.
Pasted paper, charcoal and gouache on cardboard.

LIKE every sculptor, Laurens had the habit of brushing his hand against different textures; he could grasp the formal factors in a given material, which dictate angles and inclinations, visual rhythms and thickness. This allowed him to bring a remarkable degree of attentiveness to the pasted paper; he diversified cardboard and paper textures in his two-dimensional compositions with the same fastidiousness he brought to his three-dimensional constructions. In his collages, each surface has its own tangible identity, independent of form and colour. Consider, for example, the *Woman with Mantilla* (1916): note the way the fluffy paper in the background has been folded back here and there; notice how the variously watermarked and textured scraps of different weight paper offer different resistances to the finger; observe how the colour of the strip of blue paper is structured by its mechanical texture. In addition, the artist emphasizes (with a wholly musical sensitivity) almost imperceptible accidents due to the encounter of two different materials, imperfect gluing, stray lines, folds, stains, transparent overlappings, thick layerings. For these "accidents" capture light, they bring its tremor to the work's surface (from which Cubism's analytical approach all too often banished it).

Gino Severini
(1883-1966)
Still Life with the Review *Nord-Sud*, 1917.
Pasted paper, pencil, pen and ink, gouache.

46

A LOUDER, FASTER ART

THE FUTURISTS, self-defined as "primitives w th a wholly renewed sensibility," were quick to adapt the Cubists' invention of the pasted paper to their own outlook on life. As early as 1912 a number of young painters, established members of the movement founded in 1909 by the Italian poet Filippo Tommaso Marinetti, discovered Braque's and Picasso's early experiments with this technique. The Futurists soon began to work extraneous elements into their painted compositions, though they did so less frequently and systematically than the Cubists. But while the Cubists' use of elements taken from manufactured goods cannot be dissociated from their slowly matured individual reflections on the new powers of the eye, collage as practised by the Italian painters expresses the will to break with the past, the aggressiveness, the irrepressible high spirits, and the extroverted character that typify the Futurist movement. There is something symbolic about the fact that one of the first extraneous substances included in a Futurist painting is the silver glitter on the dancer's skirt in Gino Severini's *Blue Ballerina* of 1912. Here you have all the showiness, breeziness, and casual eclecticism that was to become the hallmark of Futurism.

Such "puerile and sentimental" frivolities, as Guillaume Apollinaire called them in one of his peevish moments, were really just a superficial and ancillary expression of a whole current of thought and feeling. Nor was the author of *Alcools* himself altogether a stranger to the birth of this movement. His famous statement in defence of Picasso's first daring experiments with collage—"a painting can be made with anything you like"—is echoed by Boccioni's declaration in the *Technical Manifesto of Futurist Sculpture* (1912): "We must destroy the so-called nobility, wholly literary and traditional, of marble and bronze; and we must firmly deny the law that a sculptural ensemble must be made exclusively from one single material. The sculptor may use twenty or more different materials if he likes. . .provided that the plastic emotion requires it:. . .glass, wood, cardboard, iron, cement, hair, leather, cloth, mirrors, electric light etc." Much more self-assured and radical n their statements than their fellow painters in France (who avoided group discussions and official exhibitions and kept to themselves in their ateliers), the Futurists

led by Marinetti issued manifestoes, made public proclamations, and organized turbulent concerts and theatrical performances to publicize their declaration of war on the past, the bourgeoisie, the sublime and the romantic in art, moonlight, and Venetian tourism! Instead they celebrated the future, speed, movement, machines ("a roaring automobile. . . is more beautiful than the Victory of Samothrace"), urban landscapes, noise, crowds, electricity, and—more questionably —war.

It seemed only natural to them as artists that they should explore the throbbing, rapidly changing social and economic reality of their own times. These modern urban dwellers, witnessing technical inventions that were altering the rhythms of life, sought to express this exciting frenzy in their own works. Just as earlier generations had preferred forests and seascapes, the Futurists favoured urban settings, streets, and city squares (which inspired Marcel Duchamp to quip that Futurism was in the end merely an "urban impressionism").

One thing is certain: unlike the Cubist painters who shut out the world behind their closed studio windows, the Futurists kept their windows wide open to let in the maximum amount of simultaneous, if possible violent, fleeting, and contradictory impressions. Planes overlap and interpenetrate, colours at opposite ends of the spectrum lie side by side, lines are broken up, bisected, so as to confound visual logic and confront the beholder with the unexpected. Further, the eye loses its privileged position to the ear as the picture surface explodes into onomatopoetic cries and shouts. Even the sense of touch is brought into play with the introduction of new substances.

Choosing a "modern" subject means coming up with new plastic ideas. To this task the Futurists applied themselves eagerly. Marinetti used free verse to create a "poetry freed from its traditional constraints, one that gets its rhythms from the symphony of political meetings, factories, automobiles, airplanes in flight." Russolo anticipated concrete music when he summoned forth urban noises from his "sound machines." The Futurist painters who used collage did so with the idea of capturing the rhythms of modernity. By integrating in a painting's unitary field visual elements taken from daily modern reality, and making this

Carlo Carrà
(1881-1966)
Interventionist Demonstration, 1914.
Pasted paper, gouache and ink on cardboard.

integration express the jarring discontinuities of the urban dweller's visual experience at every hour of the day, they hoped to render the "actual dynamic sensation" (as they put it) of life's spectacle in contrast to the fixed moments of traditional painting. Now collage provokes in the reading of the art work just such interruptions of temporal and semantic continuity, if only by virtue of the harsh contouring of the artist's scissors, the relief and contrasting textures of the superadded materials, the semantic displacement of the extrapictorial information conveyed by newspaper clippings. Thus the Futurist pasted paper asserted a connection with the space outside the work; and it conducted the vibration of this external space right into the work, bringing all the clamour and urgency of the world to the picture plane through a sort of visual metonymy.

ALL the themes of Futurism are combined in this Carrà collage dated 1914. It is like a musical score suggesting the effervescence, anarchic disorder, and festiveness of an outdoor popular rally. In a vortex that conjures a blaring megaphone calling out slogans to every corner of Italy, cheers, hoots, whistlings, and the shrilling of sirens assail us with the force of an airplane propeller whirling into action. Collectively the small pasted papers resembling strips of tickertape suggest the diversity, urgency, simultaneity, and geographical reach of the news items modulated by the typography.

The repetition of certain letters draws out the sound visually. The shape and distribution of the cut-out fragments emphasize, cloak, or suspend the visual logic. Colours, forms, and signs create a dynamic, buoyant sensation that speaks not only to the eye and ear but to all of the senses, urging the viewer to take part in the crowd's rejoicing.

WAR, for Marinetti the "world's sole hygiene," is another Futurist theme Bent on overthrowing the established order and ushering in a new age of energy, the Futurists viewed struggle, including armed struggle, as a vital part of their moral and aesthetic philosophy. They saw war as the supreme expression of dynamic forces, a jubilant explosion of energies blowing away the inertia of traditionalism, a fulfilment of human personality, and a "source of tremendous creative novelty."

In 1915 Boccioni volunteered for the "queer war" that was to claim his life one year later. This 1915 collage may have been inspired by Marinetti's remark that artists should admire "the crazy sculptures our inspired artillery is carving in the enemy ranks." The violence of the cavalry charge shatters the image's realism. Lines of force, jarring planes, blurred shapes, and repetitive graphic signs confront us in what is clearly an experiment in pure plastic energy, not an attempt to depict a specific experience.

The newspaper clippings help to specify the circumstances of the picture (the battle is being waged in the mud and snow of trenches under a heavy winter sky in Alsace), but the cut-out silhouettes of the soldiers (toy figures, really) reduce the actual event to something like an inexorable, albeit pointless, exercise in which the individual combatant is merely an expendable, insignificant pawn sacrificed to the driving forces of the universe.

Umberto Boccioni
(1882-1916)
Charge of Lancers, 1915.
Tempera, ink and pasted paper on cardboard.

Fortunato Depero
(1892-1960)
Dancer for the Ballet *The Nightingale's Song,* 1916.
Pasted paper on cardboard.

cession into depth. The artist's intention is to mask the human body and its volumes behind an armour which emphasizes its articulations and mechanical construction. The dancer's lithe figure is made to wed rigid jerky lines of force which suggest the hectic rhythms of modern life and its metallic harshness. "Let the dancer pay court to machines, let him prepare the marriage of man and machine," Marinetti proclaims in his *Manifesto of the Futurist Dance* (1917).

Commissioned by Diaghilev in 1916 to design the décors for Stravinsky's ballet *The Nightingale's Song,* Depero imagined costumes consisting of triangles, cylinders, and squares. Their complex structure obliged Leonid Massine to devise a new choreography adapted to them. Thus modern ballet was enriched with a new abstract vocabulary; its dance steps, violent gestures, scenic discontinuities, strident sounds, and harsh lighting, echoed the innovations of

As EARLY as 1914 Mario Sironi (like Boccioni) embedded paper cutouts in his paintings. Apart from the fact that this technique added bright tones not found in his palette, the arrangement of the extraneous fragments helped to express the "actual dynamic sensation" that all the Futurists aimed at. Images broken down into heterogeneous elements that overlap incoherently and clumsily enabled Sironi to render the convulsive throbbing of an airplane engine, a drinker's hiccoughs, a cyclist's jarring rush over cobblestones, a plane's dizzy acrobatics, or, as here, the disjointed frenzy of limbs jerking to fast music.

The dancer's body no longer expresses the classical ideals of equilibrium and harmony but something like a jumping jack's feverish twitching. Here is an assemblage of disconnected limbs recalling the separate parts of a fragile ungainly automaton endlessly repeating its irrepressible movements. On closer examination, we begin to feel that Sironi did not share the optimistic enthusiasm of his fellow Futurists. There is something disquieting about the setting, an oppressive quality to the space enclosing the dancer. Despite the tapping heels, the syncopations of what is presumably a jazz band, and the flashing lights, there is an ominousness to the scene. The shadow of war intrudes with the inlaid newspaper clippings.

FORTUNATO Depero s discarded maquette for a ballet costume is an assemblage of small geometrical shapes traced with a square and compass on coloured papers whose flat tints counteract even the most minimal re-

Mario Sironi
(1885-1961)
Dancer, 1917.
Tempera and pasted paper on cardboard.

Giacomo Balla
(1871-1958)
Line of Speed + Landscape, 1915.
Pasted paper on cardboard.

Cubist and Futurist art. In Depero's work the dynamic vitalism of a Boccioni or a Carrà seems controlled, condensed into a concretion of forms that recall a childhood world of toys and fairy tales where what passes for reality can be taken apart and reassembled at will with no dire consequences. That is why the collages and puppets, the masks and décors, the poetry and architecture, the furniture and clothes conceived by Depero, that genial latter day "Geppetto," were in his view merely different means to attain the same goal: a total work of art combining dreams and machines, and educating the modern sensibility to a gayer, more sprightly and imaginative life.

GIACOMO BALLA painted a series of variations on "speeding automobiles" in 1913. With these kinetic paintings he gradually revolutionized the laws of pictorial representation. To render the physical reality of a moving object, he abandoned fixed points in space and time and concentrated on celebrating the object's trajectory, its perpetual flight. Not only did speed make initially discrete optical sensations (in the painting of the single viewpoint) merge into simultaneity, but it also dissolved the object's form. And so the painter soon had no choice but to express only the object's dynamic essence. Thus Balla came to abstraction less as a logical conclusion to his cogitations on the nature of appearances than through a series of experiments with technical possibilities and concretely verifiable physical laws. Later he realized that the picture plane cannot fully render the impression of volume produced on the eye by the new time factor and he began to construct "plastic-dynamic complexes" in space. He used painting and sculpture, and music and poetry, to create total works of art that expressed the multiplicity of sensations produced by the new conditions of life.

This fine 1915 collage belongs to the middle period of Balla's visual experimentation. The sharp aggressive forms boldly cut out of bright monochrome paper that resolutely eschews nuances suggest arrowlike lines of force piercing a space whose boundaries have been pushed back by time's flight. The intersecting lines, interrupted colours, overlapping forms, and the resulting slight relief (an effect special to the pasted paper technique) create an impression of volumetric transparence, a concrete plastic expression of speed, that Balla sought to recapture later in three-dimensional works like *Boccioni's Fist: Lines of Force II*.

Olga Rozanova
(1886-1918)
Aircraft over the City.
Illustration for Alexander
Kruchenykh's *War*, Petrograd, 1916.
Linocut and pasted paper.

THE POETICS OF THE ELEMENTARY

Russian Suprematism was the final outgrowth of the Cubists' attempt to record the object in its visual essence. From 1915 on, it cancelled out all reference to the outside world and left the visual space to pictorial elements alone. This clean break with reality, peculiar to the Russian mind, could not have been envisaged by Braque or Picasso, even in their most abstract compositions. But in fact this leap into the void of pure forms, achieved by Malevich in his *Black Square on a White Ground*, represents the end-result of a long reflection on the autonomy of painting, which started at the end of the eighteenth century and gained ground fast from Cézanne onwards. It meant that painting was reduced to its basic elements—lines, colours, forms—and these were now arranged on the canvas in conjunction with some added material (whereby the work qualifies as a collage) which becomes more prominent as interest in the subject dwindles.

It is this kind of investigation that artists like Kandinsky, Klee, and Mondrian devoted themselves to, focusing their energy on the power of pictorial language and on the analysis of the elements composing this new syntax. But no one seemed more determined than Malevich to eliminate any references to the past, to range beyond the boundaries of painting and reach back to the "zero level" of the visible world; the latter being understood as the "vast space of cosmic repose... a world bare of objects, facing us with the void unveiled." No one, except maybe the rebels of the Dada movement, had any similar preoccupations to those of the Moscovite painter. Coinciding in time with Malevich's theories, Dada made its appearance in Zurich and soon spread throughout the world. The passionate conviction that impelled Malevich and his disciples in their quest for a non-objective truth stemmed, on the one hand, from their longing for the absolute, their eager commitment to any spiritual endeavour reaching out beyond the world as it is; but, on the other hand, it rested on the more recent discovery of the Oriental origins of Russian art, which had never quite assimilated the rules of realistic representation based on the Western model and prescribed by the Russian court since the seventeenth century.

Thus, independently of the theoretical conflicts which opposed it to the contemporary European aesthetics (i.e. Cubism and Futurism, from which however it drew support for its principles, as also from Matisse's *Dance* and *Music* visible from 1910 in Sergei Shchukin's Moscow townhouse), the Russian avantgarde looked back to its own heritage of folk and religious art, which had remained alive wherever the imperial authority had failed to impose its conventions. Primitive painting, with its firm drawing, cut-out shapes, and unmixed colours, keeps the eye on the picture surface instead of letting it wander among the illusions of a simulated depth. This return to Russian folk art did indeed influence the painters, poets, musicians, stage producers, and choreographers at the beginning of the century. And to this group one may add collectors, publishers, and critics. They were all to express themselves within this revolutionary movement which sought to purify the artist's language and make it abstract.

Inseparable from the painters' adventure, and even anticipating it, the linguistic research of several contemporary poets into the origins and workings of the Russian language and popular speech-forms, lent support to Malevich's intuitive move towards a new visual space. Designed to break off any connection with the logical flow that had ensured the unfolding in space and time of the linear discourse, the transmental language invented by Velimir Khlebnikov and Alexander Kruchenykh, called Zaum (from *zaumnoe*, meaning transrational), disrupted the standard rhythms, subtle word-sounds, shades of meaning, and lucid structures which characterize rational syntax. Further, this metalanguage disconnected parts normally joined together, like the sign and its referent which ensure a logical compromise, the order of letters which dictates spelling, even the mechanism of verbal relationships as determined by etymology. Only present henceforth were the sounds and expressive energies contained in the fundamental units of the language, the latter now referring back to nothing but itself.

So it was only natural that the book should act as the medium between this new poetry (akin to the trance-like outpourings of religious mystics or even to inspired babytalk) and the Suprematist vision. The latter sought in the absence of objects for an upsurge of pure presence, and it was precisely the collage technique, adapted by Olga Rozanova to book illustration, which embodied this encounter of poetry and painting. It was apparently the very guiding principle behind the composition of the Suprematist picture that demanded the collage technique. So it is that the transrational constructions of Malevich, Ivan Klyun, Alexandra Exter, and Liubov Popova are characterized at this time by the combination of abstract units floating in a space no longer governed by concepts like top and bottom, before and after; a space resulting rather from an obstinate desire to transcend the usual spatial limits accepted by the eye. From now on, the image was determined by the anti-naturalistic logic of the construction, no longer by a slavish imitation of reality. Each colour plane owed its equilibrium to the relations and tensions it maintained with the surface of the canvas and the other formal elements drawn into the orbit of a process that could at any time cease or start up again. So this new rhetoric called for an intuitive intelligence impatient of the trammels of any logical proceeding; it called for a continual interchange and adaptation of the elements that went to make up the picture. What other technique could have translated this new rhetoric better than collage, whose intrinsic powers of montage and disjunction favour the overlapping, overlaying, and interpenetration of forms, while respecting the primal autonomy of each? The reduction to pure form by scissored cutouts proved an ideal way of constituting the new space championed by the Suprematists from 1915 to 1918. This device permitted a mosaic structure of small pieces of coloured paper, interacting in endless patterns of non-objective elements on the picture plane. They set in motion the shift of weight or of colour energies which, again and again, carries the eye in new directions, giving rise to ever fresh structures and dynamic breaks which can at any time be reversed or heightened. All these factors are inherent in the nature and workings of collage.

AT THE beginning of the century, women played a leading role in the renewal of Russian culture,. The great number of them who participated in intellectual activities, social actions, aesthetic reflections, and the making of original creations of the time, was impressive. Their intervention at decisive moments and their feminine sensibility seemed to influence more than once the course of events which accelerated drastically during this period. In the field of collage alone, we have the works of Olga Rozanova, Liubov Popova, Sonia Delaunay-Terk, Alexandra Exter, Varvara Stepanova, and Natalia Goncharova. One of the very first Russian collages was made by Goncharova,

Naum Granovski
(1898-1971)
Cover design for Iliazd's *Ledentu le phare*,
Paris, 1923.
Letterpress and pasted paper on cardboard.

as the cover illustration of the book by Velimir Khlebnikov and Alexander Kruchenykh, *Mirskontsa*.
There is no better illustration of the principles of the Constructivist aesthetic than this 1920 collage by Liubov Popova. Confronted by its utter sobriety, the spectator is brought face to face, above and beyond illusionist blandishments, with the essential scaffolding which permits the image to take shape. Even before grasping the picture in its totality, the eye fastens on each of the elements which account for the equilibrium of the whole: four simple legible forms, three pure colours, and the various textures of paper which add a third dimension, suggesting a palpable depth to the picture by the grain, thickness, roughness, or shine of the surfaces. But from this initial scrutiny of the material elements making up the picture, one is led at once to another stage (and this is Popova's original contribution to the furtherance of Malevich's ideas): a perception of the internal relationships which go to dynamize the surface: varying proportions of forms, energy tensions arising from their direction, weight, or tilt, harmonies and discords between interacting colour planes, juxtapositions, overlappings, and penetrations to which the artist gives the keenest attention. The visual emotion here receives a shift of emphasis: it arises now from the fullness of the spec-

Liubov Popova
(1889-1924)
Untitled, 1920.
Pasted paper.

tator's mind as, in the moment of looking, it reconstructs the mechanism which has presided over the making of the work. With its obvious cutoffs and seams, collage better than any other technique permits us to single out the successive stages of the artist's work. The eye is no longer content with an overview of the surface. It pries beneath, working its way back over the temporal sequence of the picture's making. Space here is fertilized by time.

In THE eleven collages she made in 1916 to illustrate *The Universal War*, a book of poems composed by her husband Alexander Kruchenykh in the Zaum language, Olga Rozanova put into practice, with a deft and appealing lyricism of her own, the teachings of her master, Malevich. On a blue monochrome ground, suggesting boundless space, five geometric shapes free of any reference to the real world set up a ballet which draws its stark, unadorned grace from a combination of picture elements reduced to their minimal

expression. Each form scissored out of sheets of paper of different colour and texture, seems to drift like a free and unique body let loose in the flux of spatial vastness. But each body remains independent even when caught up in the complex play of occultations, precessions, eclipses, attractions, and repulsions, which collide, interweave, and come apart in the silent spaces of an original cosmology whose random workings are more related to the future of the universe than to man's present.

Released from the discipline of perspective and recession, the eye is projected into a totally new *dynamic field*, traversed by innumerable contradictory energies; a field where the intervals of emptiness acquire at one stroke a sharply heightened plastic presence, like a sudden materialization on the picture surface of those lines of force which, according to atomic physics, give structure to the void, whose negativeness becomes creativeness. In these eleven collages for one of the finest books of the large publishing output of these years, Olga Rozanova creates a space con-

Olga Rozanova
(1886-1918)
Explosion in a Trunk.
Illustration for Alexander Kruchenykh's *Universal War*, Petrograd, 1916.
Paper and fabric collage.

Sonia Delaunay
(1885-1979)
Zenith Clock Poster, 1913-1914.
Cut and pasted paper.

stantly on the verge of breaking up, under the ever shifting impact of a multitude of vanishing points. Each one of these collage variations, turning on minute displacements of mass or colour energy, vouches for the conviction, common to most of the Russian avant-garde, that true creative originality finds its richness and power in a state of perpetual change, of stimulating instability and precariousness. The collage technique, by its very fragility, induces this mood of uncertainty and suspense.

ALTHOUGH she had left Russia in 1905, to settle in Paris with Robert Delaunay whom she married in 1910, Sonia Terk maintained close ties with the Ukraine of her childhood, whose decorative traditions were the source and stimulus behind her experiments with colour and her taste for the applied arts. Remembering the bright colours with which Ukrainian peasants decorated objects of everyday use, like furniture, fabrics, and household utensils, she took up the coll-

age technique in 1913 to decorate her bookbindings: small paper cutouts in different colours and shapes, reacting variously to the incidence of light and forming an abstract composition which no drawing could achieve, the wide range of effects arising solely from the interplay of colour contrasts. A year later she carried out a publicity project for Zenith watches, worked up from a line of verse by Blaise Cendrars, with whom she had just finished a splendid book, *La Prose du Transsibérien*, offering the reader a simultaneous perception of text and picture. In the Zenith ad it is the contrasting planes of colour which produce the dynamic compression of sonorous and visual space required by the publicity message, amplified here by the different sized letters, the bright colours, the curve of concentric shapes spreading the echo. Each piece of pasted paper having been crumpled when laid on or under the effect of the paste, the picture surface appears to quiver with flashing lights—which adds even more to the trepidation and rhythmic saturation of this creation bursting with vitality.

Hans Arp
(1887-1966)
By the Laws of Chance, 1916.
Pasted paper on cardboard.

58

BY THE LAWS OF CHANCE

Around the time that Marinetti was making his noisy declarations of war and organizing a Futurist phalanx with his comrades in Italy, a number of young artists and writers were forming a close-knit group of their own in Zurich. In 1916 they founded the Cabaret Voltaire, that small scene of impromptu, almost intimate subversion which was to play such an important role in the history of contemporary art.

Determined to have no part in the butchery that was engulfing Europe, the Zurich artists were exiles less of this or that nation than of an entire civilization. What their tumultuous behaviour expressed mainly was an urgent desire to live life to the hilt ("Dada is our intensity," wrote Tzara), hoping no doubt to fend off the threat of paralysis and gathering darkness which assailed them on all sides. The Alsatian artist Hans Arp, the German poets Hugo Ball and Richard Huelsenbeck, the Berlin painter Hans Richter, the Rumanians Marcel Janco and Tristan Tzara, and others from Switzerland, Austria, Sweden, Russia, all loudly proclaimed—punctuating their utterances with cries, dances, and "jazz noise protest"—their utter contempt for all utopian ideals that postpone the splendid authority of the present to a fictitious afterlife. Equally scornful of History which, in their view, was irremediably frozen under an icecap of dogma, they gave vent to their hatred for Reason and Progress, in whose names the most appalling acts of barbarism were being committed.

For them, the humanistic society built on the ethical foundations of work, religion, family, and fatherland was now obsolete. The framework into which man had striven for centuries to fit the world had been smashed under the repeated blows of technical and scientific revolutions, social and ethical transformations. The Dada artists wanted to supplant the successively propounded and discarded systems of the past with a new systemlessness, an indeterminate space where indolence, nonconformity, insolence, and spontaneity would produce creative chaos. They did not seek clear-cut perspectives but a "derangement of the senses" which would put man back in touch with the creative energies buried under the old precepts of the classical order. They replaced the anthropocentric view dominant since the Renaissance with a sudden relativism in perceptual relations which in turn brought about a profound modification in mental perspectives. And with this radical negation of values (a negation so radical that it became impossible to re-establish any values whatsoever), art, the loftiest expression of the individual in the humanistic tradition, was toppled from its pedestal.

Not only did Dada reject the traditional subjects and aims of art, as the Futurists had done earlier; it also redefined the artist's field of action and indeed his very function in society. For what freedom is there for the artist who has spurned the past and is indifferent to the promises of the future? Caught between choices restricted by his own rejections, he has no option but to increase and to keep increasing the intensity of the world's anarchic effervescence as it presents itself to his view. He has no choice but to foster by every available means the emergence of those particles of energy he senses beneath the shell of the quotidian. Whether it was on the stage of the Cabaret Voltaire, in the poems of Tristan Tzara, or under Hans Arp's deft touch, the Dada spirit gave itself over, independently of any logical category, to the contradictory and subterranean forces that quiver in the flux of the now. With a joy almost sacred (when it was not out of irony or in despair), poets, musicians, painters, and thinkers deferred to the only laws that still had any validity in their eyes: the incoherent, simultaneous, unpredictable laws of intuition and chance.

The way was paved by the Dada poets who began to disorganize the texture of ordinary language by doing away with the rational relations governing discourse. Hugo Ball, followed by Tzara, Schwitters, and Hausmann, broke down the hitherto uncontested relation between sign and referent and chose to celebrate each term in a chaotic and random syntax. In some of their performances, the Dada poets tried to recapture the infancy of human speech by wailing, mumbling, stuttering, shouting, breaking up words and phrases and declaiming or chanting them to primitive and exotic rhythms. On other occasions they shattered the reader's familiar responses to a text by employing signs without referents, giant letters, and graphic symbols that floated on the page's indeterminate blankness without any apparent verbal or visual connections. Tzara composed poems by cutting out words in newspaper articles, shaking them up in a hat, and putting them down in random order. Discarding the old temporal and spatial connections upon which the interchanges of every shared language are based, the Dada poets used language in a way that was uncontrolled, fragmentary, and impersonal. Theirs was a language that had no limits, no temporal dimension; it lay beyond the bounds of acquired knowledge; it rejected conventional concatenations and subdivisions. A primal manifestation of existence, it freed the artist totally, enabling him to experience with a magical, sacred fervency the emergence of crude vital energies. Before long, a number of painters followed on the heels of these new "fire thieves" and surrendered with the same receptivity to the biddings of the unconscious. Their ears attuned to the whisperings of this new world, artists like Arp, Richter, Max Ernst, Duchamp, and Schwitters focused their sensibilities on the explosive creative potential that lies dormant in the quotidian, the incongruous, the adventitious. Forgoing noble materials and lofty artistry, they appropriated whatever came to hand, with, however, a marked preference for manufactured articles that exhibit no trace of the human (and inevitably too personal) hand: newsprint, wrapping paper, glass, wallpaper (already utilized by the Cubists), and scraps and refuse such as tram tickets, restaurant bills, stamps, banknotes, cinema tickets. Scissors enabled these artists to create crisp clear-cut images from which any sentimentality was pared away.

In some of his 1915 collages, Arp even went as far as using a trimmer, thus eliminating any trace of his own touch, in an attempt to "approach the pure effulgence of reality." The arbitrary element in the artist's personal sensibilities was displaced by another, more attractive arbitrariness, that of machines, or unfeeling mechanisms designed to cut, trim, fold, sew, and adjust. Paste was an admirably indifferent labour-saving expedient when it came to creating compositions of forms and colours. Rather than arranging these elements according to his own volition, the Dada artist believed that he should let them find their own positions on the canvas. He wanted them to be governed solely by the combinations of chance (which is simply life in its original state); better yet he wanted to replace pigments and impasto with readymade substances. Substances that contributed their own specific beauty to unpremeditated juxtapositions. From the tactile clash of different surfaces, the startling arrangements of forms, the ambiguous convergence of absurdities, a precarious and indefinite equilibrium would emerge; and this would be the Dada artist's response to the anxious joy he experienced as he faced the ephemeral adventure of his creation.

IN HIS first collages of 1915, Hans Arp fashioned small random constructions using pieces of paper cut from sheets of variously coloured and textured paper. Ignoring what he now saw as useless and obsolete canons of taste and sensibility, he arranged them according to the "laws of chance." The very indetermination of these images, which have neither centre, nor perspective, nor any criteria other than their own gratuitousness and total anonymity, can be viewed as an attempt to go beyond the constraints of rational thought and history and return to a free state of nature. Here life might surge forth in all its primitive force. It is this bare, elementary, Edenlike setting that Arp's concrete art unfolds. The spectator's eye is engaged solely by accidents produced by the work's splendidly unrestrained emergence, such as irregularities in the mechanically cut-out shapes, the grain of different textures, infinitesimal reliefs produced by overlapping scraps, the haphazard interplay of colours that match here, clash there. And even the semblance of order that comes from the artist's use of paste looks as if it might collapse at any moment like a stack of cards.

Hans Arp
(1887-1966)
Untitled, 1915.
Pasted paper.

Paul Joostens
(1889-1960)
Dada Abstraction, 1922.
Pasted paper on cardboard.

SWEPT in the turmoil of his age, Paul Joostens participated, like many of his contemporaries, in a number of artistic movements before taking up (under Schwitters' influence) the Dada practice of cultivated aimlessness. In his *Dada Abstraction* we are struck by the clashing textures of the collaged substances. The poetry of this accumulation of discarded, wrinkled, stained scraps of paper and cardboard (to which are added bits of utilitarian sandpaper and copperfoil) resides in the conjunction of random forms, and in the randomly selected substances that are crudely combined in a wilful surrender to the basic components of the image. Yet despite the fact that this *Dada Abstraction* gives a palpable expression to the instability and confusion of a world that is as chaotic as an un-regulated mechanism, it also suggests that seemingly valueless random combinations do constitute an order comparable to the mind's considered geometries. Thus, even as he strives to do away with any personal touch that might conceivably betray an aesthetic intention, any attempt to influence the order of the universe, the Dada artist cannot prevent an ordering, a very minimal ordering, from occurring on the heels of his decision not to intervene personally in the work. It is by no means the least paradox of the Dada adventure (but is there not a paradox in the movement's very name?) that, in a complete reversal of its premises, it generated works that have on occasion been confused with the most elaborate creations of the rational mind.

Kurt Schwitters
(1887-1948)
Picture with Light Centre, 1919.
Pasted paper and oil on cardboard.

A PRIMITIVE'S CLASSICAL ENERGY

THE THING that strikes one first about Kurt Schwitters' collages (those intimate little dramas) is how delicate they are, how refined the artist's touch is, how for d his eye. One is surprised to come across qualities like these in the work of that taciturn, neatly dressed giant of a man who spent his days wandering about with a satchel slung over his shoulder into which he would stuff an assortment of paper scraps, bits of string and rags gathered on the sidewalk or in weed-infested lots. Thanks to that good samaritan this detritus was rescued from the indifference of passers-by and the vagaries of weather. Van Gogh, more than thirty years earlier, had already shown a liking for discarded objects: rusty stoves, worn-out shoes, saucepans, chests, crates scarred by a lifetime of shifting fortunes. By depicting their indigence in his canvases, he had dignified them to a startling degree, one that no school, not even the most naturalistic school, had previously dared to envisage.

But Schwitters committed an even graver offence against the spirit of idealism when he set about systematically replacing brushes and paint tubes, chromatic values, impasto and washes, with wretched bits of detritus collected on the street. He permanently set aside the satisfactions of mastery and the seductions of imitation, and instead used glue and nails to affix to canvas or cardboard emblems of the age's decrepitude. In so doing, he carried the pasted paper revolution begun by the Cubists to its ultimate conclusion. He gives one the impression that he is fil ing in holes rather than assembling materials. It is as if he were desperately striving to stop a disintegrating world from escaping through a breach in reality.

The most striking thing about the novel "dialogue" between the German artist and his material is the crudeness of the assemblages, the seams revealing discontinuities, the hinges, the overlappings, the differences in grain and thickness, the traces of glue, the small rips with their tale of artistic effort pitted against resistant materials. Though the eye is init ally caught by the poverty, the wear and tear, the multiple deteriorations the materials have suffered before be ng chosen by the artist, yet his work produces an impression of rare harmony. A rough sense of structure gradually emerges at the centre of what seems to be a precarious disorder. The fact is that, while the fragments taken from the external world—the world of the quotidian and of history—possess a specific shape, colour, and texture, and while the materials generally bear indications, letters, numbers which define a direction, suggest an anecdote, or refer to a price, place, or date, they nevertheless lose whatever exact value or contingency they may initially have had the minute they are appropriated in the act of composing the work. Indeed, the quality of the materials themselves is unimportant. Anything that addresses itself to the eye will do. It hardly matters even what intentions lie behind the crucial interaction of hand and eye. All that matters is the dazzling encounter between the artist's instincts and the ephemeral, limited propositions of the substances which vehicle a circumstantial randomness.

But if Schwitters willingly surrenders to the ebb and flow of the innumerable contradictory energies that pulse through the world, he continues to be deeply interested in the distribution of the parts, the crystalline patterns of free associations, ephemeral conjunctions, dazzling shortcuts or occultations. The classicism of this true revolutionary rests on a formal enshrining of materials in the art work, on a quest for an equilibrium that respects the existing tensions between an outer indeterminacy and an inner necessity. There is nothing really surprising about the suspended state the viewer experiences when he contemplates one of Schwitters' collages. The artist's entire oeuvre, his entire life, oscillates between a disturbing strangeness (the eccentricity all his biographers have remarked on) and the fundamental naturalness of a man for whom even the smallest gesture, even the most trivial utterance, whether social or poetic, has a place in the absolute logic of his art. The Berlin Dadaists were quick to perceive this ambivalence and denied Schwitters admittance to their group. Though they admired the way this quiet man "nailed his paintings together," they had no understanding for the spirit of discipline and the yearning for harmony which guided him. Schwitters does not demolish, he collects. He rarely uses scissors and their accusing vindicative strokes; he sits back and lets time, passing events, the modern metropolis, and new industrial techniques act on the materials unassisted. To him this seems a sufficiently tragic process to obviate the need for his own intervention. Schwitters is concerned with building —this is clear throughout his life—if only building on the ruins of the present, if only building *with* ruins. Building and assembling.

His intense activity after the end of the First World War, in fields as different as poetry, drawing, collage, assemblages, architecture, drama, and publishing (with a creative freedom and energy equalled only by his renewed zest for living) had one single aim: to produce an all-encompassing work which would successfully integrate even the most disparate elements. Schwitters dreamed daily of this total work of art, this Merz cathedral (Merz being the artist's term for his own art in contrast to the destructive ventures of Berlin Dada), this passionate attempt to harmonize opposites. It was a dream sustained by the hope of seeing the frontiers that divide the arts, languages, and men vanish once and for all.

Kurt Schwitters
(1887-1948)
Cover of *Die Kathedrale*, 1920.
Lithograph from a set of eight.

THE MOTIFS and the overall concept of the collage *with red 4* (c. 1919) are still drawn from the dry, precise mechanical repertoire used by Dada artists of all tendencies. It was less the dynamic sensation of movement the Futurists were so fond of that fascinated artists like Max Ernst in Cologne, Grosz in Berlin, Duchamp and Picabia in New York, than the peculiar cold beauty of pistons and valves, the physical satisfaction the eye derives from gears, axles, cranks, transmission belts. A machine's parts are clearly intelligible, but they are combined in relations of increasing complexity which lead to a coherent, logical result. At this stage, however, the Dada spirit intervenes and throws the mechanism out of kilter. It distorts the original concept. In some cases (for example Duchamp), a ''bachelor machine'' vainly repeats its impotent action; in others (Picabia), the mechanism is shattered by the contradictions of non-art; and in still others (Max Ernst), machines enable the artist to combine wholly incompatible areas of reality in the same scene. As for Schwitters, he takes isolated mechanical components and, with a childlike sense of play enhanced by a wonderful sense of humour, sets them dancing to

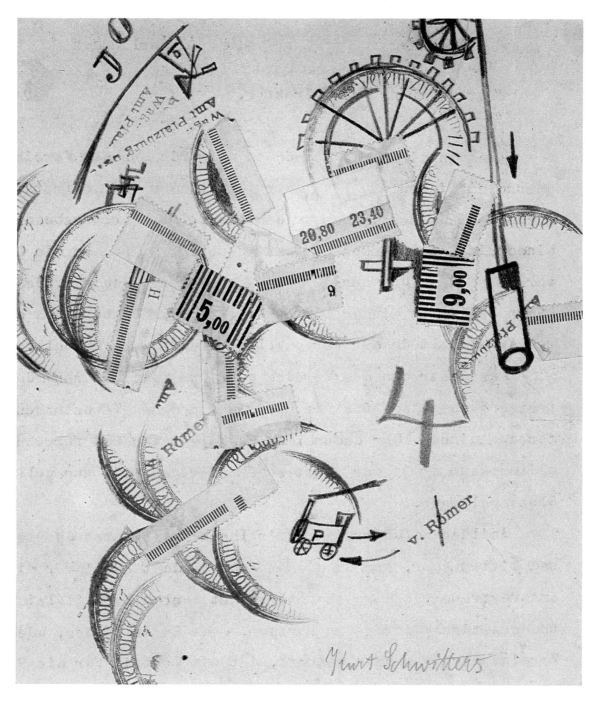

Kurt Schwitters
(1887-1948)
with red 4, c. 1919.
Stamping, pencil, pasted paper.

the frail tune of a music box. A tenuous thread links the separate parts revolving to a rhythm of tiny jerky movements. Schwitters (who was originally an industrial draughtsman) breaks down the blueprint rigidity of the drawing and accentuates the movement by stamping it repeatedly with a round seal. Collaged strips of stamped paper give this shaky construction a flimsy and rather ironic framework. But at the same time the collage establishes a spatio-temporal rapport between the different elements of the image. The wholly or partially overlapping cancellations present the eye with visual non-sequiturs, but nevertheless suggest a temporal sequence to the mechanical action. This produces an impression of transparency, of an unimpeded circulation between outside and inside, before and after, the whole and the parts.

Kurt Schwitters
(1887-1948)
Drawing A2: Hansi-Schokolade, 1918.
Pasted paper.

COMBINING new techniques and traditional procedures, the important 1919 collage entitled *Picture with Light Centre* (page 62) attempts to achieve a comparable fusion of opposites. The tension produced by the contradictory lines, intersecting planes, contrasting textures and thicknesses, not to mention the collision of extremely diverse and ephemeral bits of information, resolves into an abstract landscape possessing great inner radiance. It is as though the manifold outer reality had suddenly undergone a terrific acceleration: forms and colours are blurred, and the spectator is projected into a four-dimensional space where his own position and angle of vision are abruptly relativized.

ONE of Schwitters' earliest collages, *Drawing A2: Hansi-Schokolade* is in all probability a tribute to Hans Arp (hence the discreet allusion, "Hansi"). It illustrates in an exemplary fashion the process of transformation affecting the radically new material of the artist's vocabulary; a process that consists in stripping away the anecdotal from items found in the street so as to enhance the work's formal unity. The pleasing distribution of the parts results in the radiant authority of the whole. The tranquilly distributed coloured surfaces, the clean edges of the forms, the restful equilibrium of the volumes expresses the "intuitive will" that always guided the artist in his endeavour to bring order to randomness. Yet though the threat of the anecdotal, of the signed and dated private experience, is absorbed, the composition does not succeed entirely in wresting the materials from the violence and poverty of the outer world. The folds, worn spots, wrinkles, stains, scratch marks (all those little scars) weight the picture plane with a perception of onrushing time and the Angst of a troubled epoch.

Schwitters' collages speak to the sense of touch as well as to the eye, perhaps more so. Each scrap of paper that contributes to the image's formation stimulates a different perception. The collages offer an array of sensations that goes from the rough to the smooth, the astringent to the greasy, the soft to the hard, with a variety of intermediate perceptions diversely com-

Kurt Schwitters
(1887-1948)
Forms in Space, 1920.
Paper and fabric collage on cardboard.

bining abrasive, absorbing, repulsive, and attractive textures. Seconded by the sense of touch, the eye penetrates a space where the illusion of depth is no longer suggested by perspective, as it is in traditional art, but seems to arise from immediate sensory experience.

BETWEEN 1919 and 1921 Schwitters composed a series of "urban" collages which amalgamate in a sort of dense, confused precipitation all the spoils the artist collected in his tireless peregrinations through the city.

These works evoke the plural universe of the sidewalk with all its contrasts, its neon signs flashing bursts of garish light, its shouted multilingual advertisements in Roman and Gothic script, in numbers and emblems; its falling securities and rising stocks; its traffic; its medley of prohibitions, passports, newspapers being printed, distributed, and going stale daily; its timetables, addresses, cupidities. All this noisy chaos spills pell-mell into Schwitters' works. Worn, heteroge-

neous fragments that a few drops of glue affix to a support, they are like entries in a journal recording a modern city dweller's hard-working, dizzying life. What is more, the disparate arrangement of the materials provides a paradigmatic illustration of the complex relationships governing modern society. Cloudless for the few, these relationships are brutal, difficult, cut-and-dry for the many. Often they are mandatory, if not authoritarian; they may be futile or venal, silent or voluble, intimate or official; they are never lasting, but are invariably swept by the frantic whirlwinds that agitate society, forever driving men to reach out beyond their limits.

And yet, again, Schwitters shows us that his intention is not to glorify disorder, but to use it to recompose a new cosmology of the trivial, to reveal the irrefutable presence of a creative rigour beneath the froth of the quotidian. *Formen im Raum* (Forms in Space) proclaims the title of this 1920 collage. The accent is, as always, on the task of formal reconstruction. What we have here is a sidewalk, of course, but it is a reorganized sidewalk!

Raoul Hausmann
(1886-1971)
The Art Critic, 1919-1920.
Collage of photographs, illustrations and paper.

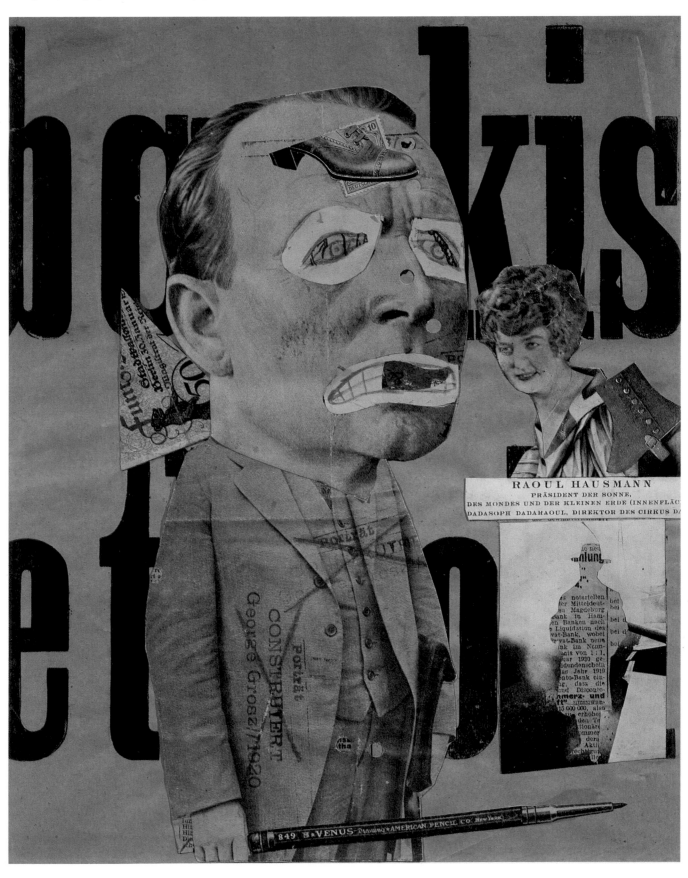

BROADSIDES AND MANIFESTOES

THE Dada ideas which evolved from 1916 on in neutral Switzerland, that "island of life surrounded by an ocean of death" (as Hans Richter expressed it) where a group of artists forgathered in Zurich around Hugo Ball and Tristan Tzara, were then transplanted by Richard Huelsenbeck to Berlin. There, confronted with the tragic reality of a nation caught in the maelstrom of war, they acquired a decidedly more violent character. Disillusionment, hunger, and social injustice were rife in the German capital where the spectacle of dire poverty, casualties from the front, and broken families daily brought home the horror of a savage and senseless conflict. In such a setting, the rejection of traditional art, the provocative stance and the outbursts of primitive energy that had been freely vented in Zurich's Cabaret Voltaire crystallized into an overt, concrete revolt.

At the Berlin Dada Club founded early in 1918 by Huelsenbeck and his circle (Hausmann, Herzfelde, Baader, Grosz, and Heartfield), the rejection of traditional values developed into a fierce struggle against the establishment. No longer were the new intellectual forces emerging in creative minds confined to the domain of pure aesthetics; now they were directed aggressively against those who were deemed responsible for the failure of civilization: the military and the bourgeoisie. In the prevailing atmosphere of despair and confusion, rendered gloomier still by the failure of revolutionary hopes in 1918-1919 (hopes most of the Dadaists had themselves entertained) and the return to power of the old ruling clique, artists no longer had the leisure to pose as dandies and engage in abstruse intellectual discussions. Their moral indignation had, they felt, to be harnessed to the cause of the disinherited and oppressed. In a word, they saw themselves as soldiers of the Revolution. The irony they cultivated, their flair for scandal, their contemptuous rejection of father figures and History, found an outlet in concrete action.

Since none of the prescriptions of traditional art was of the slightest use to the Dada artists, and since the concepts of humanistic culture had failed to stop the fratricidal bloodshed, they made it their mission to sever the few remaining ties that linked them to the discredited idealisms and crippling introspection of the pre-war years. Their sense of urgency and their revulsion drove them into the street, where they denounced and mocked the deceptions and broken promises of politicians. They used deliberately ugly, and provocative images to reveal the ignominy of those who obstinately refused to see that reason was foundering and that they themselves were responsible for this state of affairs.

To carry out their program of spiritual cleansing and to open eyes sealed by propaganda and habit, the German Dadaists required a more incisive tool than the caricaturist's pencil, a more effective vocabulary than woodcutting, which had traditionally been used for social protest in Germany. Their weapon, sufficiently rapid and powerful to answer the thunder of guns, was collage; more specifically, the collage of photoengravings, in other words photomontage, a Dada invention that dates from this time.

There were several reasons why scissors and paste seemed ideally suited to the Dada campaign of protest. They sped up the production of art works, and, by limiting the artist's role to that of an assembler, they democratized the act of creation. Collage was the perfect technique for shattering the "illusion" of polished workmanship. It brought picture-making down to earth. It announced a return to dilettantism and an end to the concept of creation dominated by the vanity of bourgeois artists. It gave a voice to the instincts buried under the Dadaist's *bête noire* of idealistic learning. Moreover it presented the eye with brutal, inelegant, even obscene discontinuities. Thus it was an effective instrument for undermining an obsolete reality and was well adapted to the program these committed artists had originally set for themselves.

In selecting images from printed sources, exploiting the illustrations in daily newspapers and mass-circulation magazines (an incomparable reservoir of popular fantasies), the Dadaists hoped to carry their enterprise of sabotage to the heart of the fraudulent bourgeois "truth." They carved, cut up, sliced, and eviscerated this material; they then recomposed a plausible coherence wherein overlays, contrasts, disproportions, shocking conjunctions and disjunctions, mutilations and farcical combinations expressed the confusion of a society unable to cope with its ills otherwise than by violence. In doing so, their intention was clearly to rub salt in already festering wounds. They made collage a language that was both savage and readily accessible to the masses, one that revealed the true face of bourgeois selfishness and profiteering, its lust for power, its dishonesty. Utilizing all materials without distinction and assembling them in what amounted to spontaneous, ephemeral demonstrations—shouts in the forms of leaflets, posters, or book wrappers—this radical and aggressive technique manifested the Dada artist's determination to bring art closer to life. The tragic clairvoyance of their critique proved powerless to stop a new, even more terrible barbarism, one that was to confirm their worst fears. But their view of the artist's role in society anticipated many expressions of contemporary art, from performances to installations, from the iconoclastic rage of the New Realists to the minimal events of Arte Povera.

HANNAH Höch, the only woman in the Berlin group, had her own approach to photomontage, a technique she discovered in 1918 under the same circumstances as Raoul Hausmann with whom she was living at the time. "In almost every home one saw an oleograph hanging on the wall. To give this image a personal touch, a photographic portrait of the absent soldier was pasted over the engraved face: I saw in a flash that I could make pictures entirely composed of cut-out photographs" (Raoul Hausmann). In Höch's

work, political militancy and a scathing criticism of established values are somewhat overshadowed by endlessly subtle combinations of heterogeneous elements. The process of dislocation is carried out with the aid of a rhetorical system of allusions, echoes, and references directed less at unmasking falsehood than at expressing in an amused manner and as if with a glancing indirectness the complexity within each one of us. In the *Bourgeois Newlyweds (Quarrel)*, a quarrel doubtless sparked by a thing as trivial as a choice of kitchen implements (but is the hankering for grinders, mills, and cleavers all that innocent?), the photographic materials clipped from contemporary magazines and catalogues are arrayed in such a way (i.e. the large slanted or overturned letters, the bursts of colour, the breaks in visual continuity, the constrained and contradictory movements of the two protagon-

ists) that they concretely express a violent argument and a couple's struggle to disentangle the inextricable knot imprisoning them in a conflict.

DAUM MARRIES is the enigmatic title of this Grosz collage, fortunately elucidated by the subtitle: *Daum Marries her pedantic automaton George in May 1920, to the great delight of John Heartfield. Metamech. Constr. after Prof. Hausmann.* Daum, we discover from other sources, is in fact the anagram of Maud, the pseudonym of the girl whom the artist did actually marry in 1920. Such private joking allusions were common in Dada circles, as were coded messages and confidential puns which could be understood only by the Club's initiates.

Grosz's legendary ferocity is tempered here by a solid dose of humorous self-scrutiny. The artist depicts himself as an elegant automaton being solicited by a streetwalker who is generously displaying her wares. The collaged elements inscribe a troubling fantasy on the rectilinear landscape of an empty city frozen in a metaphysical silence. Skilfully combined with water-colour in a rapport of trompe-l'oeil realism, the pasted papers expose the spurious transparency of the female figure by designating the artifices that bolster her seductiveness. Thus, in spite of the automaton's eminently respectable attire, they reveal the machinery of masculine desire. In addition, two collages at window level suggest the tranquil, idyllic daydreams of the city's inhabitants in the shelter of their dwellings. So overwhelmingly melancholy is Grosz's outlook on things that the artist now views the world as a stage whereon even the joyous occasions that happen to come his way are depicted as parodies of real life.

WITH his friend Johannes Baader (most of whose daring and gratuitous acts have unfortunately vanished without a trace), Raoul Hausmann representd the spirit of Berlin Dada at its purest. He was a poet, philosopher, critic, dancer, photographer, and inventor. As an artist, he was exceptionally sensitive to the multiple contradictory currents, the tremendous, often incomprehensible energies that assailed him and his contemporaries. His was an age of ferment, he felt, and the new artistic generation's radical questioning of the world was but a reflection of the prevailing chaos.

The invention of photomontage can be attributed to Hausmann less by reason of the dates and contemporary accounts that are so often cited as proofs of this than by virtue of his extraordinary talent for creating new forms of language. In this 1919-1920 "pasted picture," another name for photomontage in Berlin (page 68), an initial layer of cutting and pasting sub-

verts the proportions and perspective, thus breaking down the all too familiar visual order. A second layer of montage (the eyes and the overly large grimacing mouth pasted over the figure's own mouth and eyes, as if to stress the importance of these organs) brings the artist's malaise right into the centre of the image. The portrait is further defined by a series of summarily cut-out additions, allusions to money, fashion, women, the war, and high finance. These are distributed around the figure of the critic carrying his over-size pencil. In a vastly ironic touch, the artist's signature appears in print, and the words *Constructed Portrait George Grosz 1920* are stamped twice on the critic's body. The background is a phonetic poem by Raoul Hausmann. A few emphatic lines drawn with a red pencil complete this hastily constructed image dispatched with a blithe disregard for "good taste" and indifference towards the materials employed.

Is Hausmann's collage only (as historians have always maintained) a caricature of an art critic blind to reality and insensitive to the new language of art, a paper tiger who rushes from one gallery opening to another, chasing forever after the frivolous? Is it not possible to discern in this ambiguous image an emblematic portrait of the new artist whose freshly opened eyes are fixed with terror and anger on the sores that disfigure society? The portrait's vague resemblance to George Grosz and the fact that this artist's name occurs twice in the image inevitably suggest the most famous of the opponents of traditional art active in Berlin around 1920. Grosz, whose oddly disconnected body appears to express something of the inner confusion that tormented him all his life; whose eyes, boggling at the spectacle of human misery, brooded on the moral shortcomings of his generation; whose art expressed itself with a causticity that made no concessions, and whose favourite weapon —a pencil—tirelessly stigmatized the world of money, sex, and warmongering.

A CLOSE friendship and a complete identity of views existed between George Grosz and John Heartfield. The two artists collaborated on a number of Dada collages, and they co-signed numerous manifestoes (for example, *The Scoundrel of Art*, which was directed against the "reactionary Kokoschka"). They both detested the bourgeoisie and both joined the German Communist Party in 1919. Both believed that the artist's role consisted essentially in furthering the ideals of the proletarian Revolution, not in satisfying selfish interests rendered futile by the cruelty and urgency of the times. And yet, whereas Grosz's radically pessi-

mistic vision encompassed all of humanity, Heartfield was able to identify his enemy swiftly and precisely. Thus each time he attacks capitalism, Nazi bellicosity, or even Hitler himself, hope for a better world—a hope that burned brightly all his life—immediately re-emerges by implication.

The extraordinary power of these images produced with meticulous care on an editing table rests on a few simple principles. Conceiving of photomontage as an effective instrument of class struggle, Heartfield wanted its language to be direct, telling, and easily understood. He wanted it to strike cleanly into the heart of deception. Photography, a modern, universal technique, satisfied the first of these requirements. To satisfy the second, Heartfield soon abandoned the characteristic Dada syntax of violent discontinuities and chose instead to construct clearly legible images

having every appearance of a plausible reality, but, by virtue of the Latin tag *in cauda venenum*, resolving themselves in a startling reversal of meaning. Thus a grinning banker discloses a set of hyena's fangs, the domes of a church turn out to be warheads inscribed with hateful emblems, the branches of a Christmas tree bend at right angles to form a sinister swastika. Using visual analogies, verbal metaphors, and illuminating juxtapositions of motifs, Heartfield composed, from 1920 until the Nazis seized and destroyed it, a profoundly disturbing contemporary Book of Metamorphoses, from which comes this Nazi octopus with its evil tentacles. Heartfield transformed Grosz's aesthetics of ugliness into the "revolutionary beauty" which Aragon hailed and which has not ceased to exert an influence on photographers, protest artists, and advertising designers.

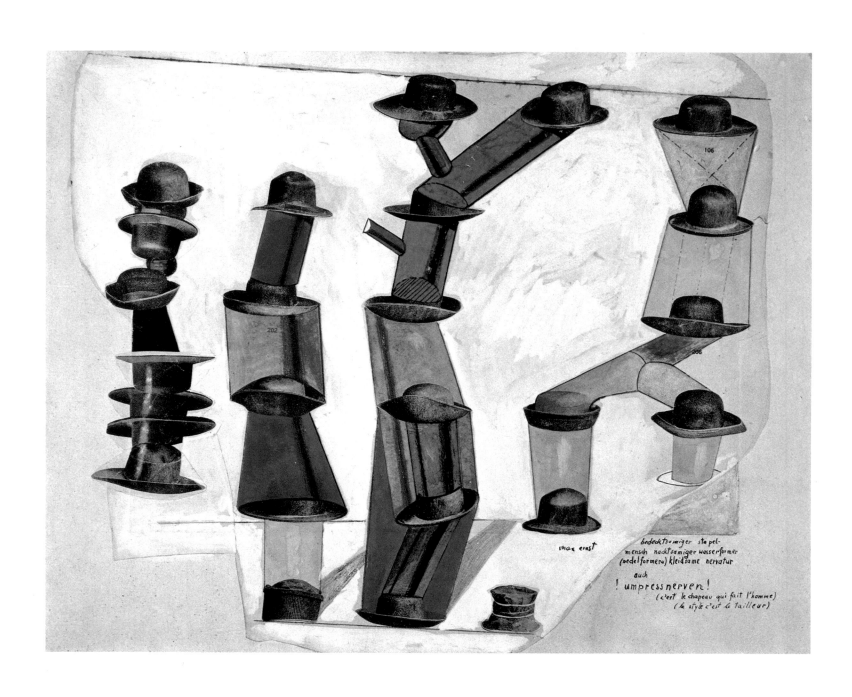

Max Ernst
(1891-1976)
The Hat Makes the Man, 1920.
Collage, pencil, pen and ink, watercolour

USING LOGIC TO SUBVERT LOGIC

"Max Ernst died on 1 August 1914. He returned to life on 11 November 1918 under the guise of a young man who wanted to become a magician and discover the myth of his times." The tone is set from the start: humour and poetry, a sense of urgency, as well as a craving for absolutes and a thirst for freedom fuel the revolt simmering "inside that restless brain." Following demobilization, the former medical student, an ardent reader of philosophy and poetry, founded a "Dada House" with his friend Johannes T. Baargeld. With the aim of awakening the conscience of their fellow citizens and reminding them that art is more than "a postprandial nap," the two artists organized several provocative exhibitions in art institutions where "serious" works were displayed alongside drawings by mental patients, African carvings, and assemblages that challenged every aesthetic convention. Undismayed by the public's total lack of comprehension, Ernst promptly set about establishing international ties with members of other Dada centres of subversion in Zurich, New York, and Paris.

As early as 1919 Max Ernst took up collage. Like Schwitters in Hanover, and Hausmann, Grosz, and Heartfield in Berlin, he used it to call reality into question. (No other technique allowed these artists to vent the anger and confusion within them as effectively.) But there was one important difference. Schwitters collected his materials in the street and then combined them in fragile constructions which were attempts to patch up the torn fabric of the present. The Berlin Dadaists stigmatized social hypocrisy by taking scissors to illustrated newspapers and savagely cutting them up. Max Ernst chose a more discreet approach. His technique for undermining reality seems unspectacular in comparison, but each time he combines figurative elements that have nothing in common and are without any inherent poetic value, and associates them in hitherto unheard of combinations, the effect is always extraordinarily disruptive. "One rainy day in 1919. . . my excited gaze was provoked by the pages of an illustrated catalogue that advertised objects for anthropological, microscopical, psychological, minerological, and palaeontological classroom demonstrations. I discovered combinations of figurative elements so remote from one another that their very absurdity provoked in me an intensification of my

faculties of sight—a hallucinatory succession of contradictory images, double, triple, multiple images that superposed on one another with the swiftness and persistence of erotic memories or drowsy visions." This helps us to understand to what extent chance plays a role in shaping Ernst's oeuvre. It acts less as an iron law than as an overall factor (like the Greek *kairos*) favouring the emergence of opportunities that the artist feels he must grasp. Faced with elements which are utterly alien to one another, mute amorphous elements, useless in their crippling isolation, the artist continues to exercise the privilege of setting off, simply by the choices he makes, the explosive charge embedded in each particle of reality.

The collage principle in Ernst's work rests on his determination to create a maximally disturbing reading of the image while minimally distorting the network of signs that make up that image. This is why Ernst tends to select his materials from a repertory of readymade images—images that have previously been reproduced elsewhere and are therefore reassuringly familiar: collotypes, engraved vignettes, scientific plates complete with their own captions. The high seriousness and precise draughtsmanship of these illustrations, which preclude any private interpretation, provide a rational, particularly fertile terrain for the imagination. The artist manipulates this material with a perverseness that is especially convincing inasmuch as he subverts its logic with logical means and uses the most commonplace objects to create a deeply troubling atmosphere. What is more, he is careful to suppress every trace of the collage process itself, so that the freely combined elements produce an intense illumination in the spectator's mind. Any glue stains and seams between fragments that might reveal a break in the image's narrative continuity are suppressed. Nothing is allowed to impinge on the illusion. This concern with keeping his touch invisible led Max Ernst to prefer flat photographic reproductions and printed plates to his original collages with their all but imperceptible reliefs.

It is only at second glance, after our eye has become entrapped in appearances, as it were, that we begin to experience the chaos of illusions in a Max Ernst collage. The homogeneous, yet indecipherable syntax of dreams is projected onto the sheet of paper by means of a series of formal substitutions, substitutions of contents, permutations of visual clues, repetitive cadences, exaggerated rhythms, suppressions, cruel or ambiguous transparencies. And, as is often the case in the a-logical realm of Hypnos, an invisible resis-

$$\sin \alpha \cdot \log (R\&H)^{dada} < \sqrt{juno}$$

Max Ernst
(1891-1976)
Plate from *Fiat Modes: Pereat Ars*, 1919.
Lithograph from a set of eight.

▷ Katharina Ondulata, 1920.
Collage, gouache and pencil.

tance hampers movement: corseted figures are encumbered with harnesses and straps or attached to pulleys, levers, switch bars; their bodies are constricted, unable to move of their own accord. Alternatively, they seem to drift off into space; they float in a disproportionate perspective that recedes towards infinity or is suddenly contracted, shallow, like the breathing of a sleeper struggling to escape from a nightmare. The sense of a malaise, if not anguish, that emanates from these images is akin to that perplexity the mind experiences before a puzzling rebus. But a rebus, once deciphered, loses its ability to tease us, whereas Max Ernst's dissection/associations continue to intrigue even after we have succeeded in piercing some of their mystery.

Further increasing this effect of baffling displacement, the titles of Ernst's collages, usually written in the mar-

gin of the work, combine (in a deliberately contrived confusion that echoes the image's warped order) fragments of aphorisms, commonplace sayings, pithy definitions, similes, and false etymologies which suggest a plurality of interpretations, but yield no single certainty.

Actually, the impression of something plausibly unfamiliar, close but unattainable, which typifies Max Ernst's early work in Cologne derives from the art of trompe-l'oeil: wooing the spectator's eye by rational means in order to undermine both reality and the act of seeing itself (in spite of the fact that this act assigns limits to reality). Max Ernst was later to render this plunge into the nether-visible—which is also a descent into the interior of the visible—even more productive and risky after he settled in Paris and became involved with the Surrealist poets.

By THE early 1920s the mechanics of desire and the mechanics of dreaming had become ubiquitous themes in the art world. Max Ernst was not only the first to deal with them; he also brought them to a state of incandescence that was unequalled by any of his contemporaries. The 1920 collage *Katharina Ondulata* is clear proof of this, in spite of the fact that its brilliant chromatic and plastic rendering of the erotic theme suggests a parody of love rather than a celebration of its mysteries. The image shows a pretentious masculine machine, akin to a rooster bristling its feathers, striving with ridiculous, futile jerky movements to reach a gorgeous coral mouth shining like a cruel comet in the pearly sky. How does Max Ernst go about translating into his novel idiom this erotic topos which is as old as the world? First, he arrays his little conqueror in a garish piece of material.

He next assembles the cut-out fragments in an emblematic figure frozen in an impotent, vainly repeated gesture. Then he isolates this figure, removing it from any kind of spatial continuity, by placing it in front of a perspectiveless landscape taken from a geological atlas: the eye is cast adrift and sinks into a non-Euclidean void. Finally, with his vibrant brush dipped in the most delicate tints, he suggests a bizarre complicity between the divorced couple. He estab-lishes connections that bridge their mutual solitude, playing on the tension between the forms and the incongruous signs until at last the explosive charge within the image is released with maximum effect. And yet, the irony enveloping the figures is so potent that it radiates outwards beyond the picture's margins to the rough filigree of the frame. And the frame's decorative pretentiousness in turn destroys any certitude the spectator may have formed about the image.

In Cubist compositions, the function of pasted papers is to reintroduce the weight of reality in a representation that is threatened with becoming estranged from the real. Collage as practised by Max Ernst proceeds in a diametrically opposite direction. Here the strips of wallpaper help to divest the image of its reality. The carefully worked out arrangement of the collaged fragments serves to disrupt any mimetic rapport that would keep the self-enclosed system of the work and the spectacle of the outer world on the same footing.

Max Ernst
(1891-1976)
Max Ernst's Bedroom Is Worth
Spending a Night In, c. 1920.
Collage heightened with gouache and pencil.

THE origins of this assault on realistic poetics are articulated in a collage dating from the same period, *Max Ernst's Bedroom Is Worth Spending a Night In*. The title is unusually explicit and its meaning goes well beyond Ernst's customary erotic irony. For there is little doubt that the artist's bedroom was, throughout his life, the scene of tremendous mental and sensory activity. It was here, in this laboratory and theatre of reveries, desires, and anxieties that Ernst was visited in his childhood by hallucinations which revealed to him the existence of strange, plural realities, abnormal states camouflaged in the midst of appearances. It was here too, in this enclosed space, this hothouse where the mind's obsessions blossomed, that the artist, gazing at catalogue illustrations, at the weird shapes on the wooden panels of a closet, at floorboards and stains on the wall, was later to invent new techniques to express his unusually sharp sense perceptions. Thus frottage was born, and Ernst's collage. In the hands of this artist gifted with a truly remarkable receptivity to the promptings of matter, these techniques became "hypersensible and rigorously exact instruments," tools that were capable of transcribing the richness and complexity of the unsuspected worlds which make up the visible realm. They could combine on the same plane, in optical constellations

le chien qui chie le chien bien coiffé malgré les difficultés du terrain causées par

une neige abondante la femme à belle gorge la chanson de la chair / max ernst

Max Ernst
(1891-1976)
The Song of the Flesh, c. 1920.
Collage and pencil over a photograph.

Plate from *Fiat Modes: Pereat Ars,* 1919.
Lithograph from a set of eight.

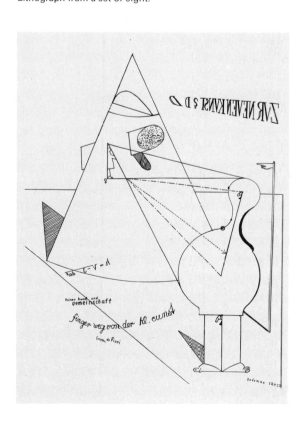

of incredible density, fields that "hoary Reason" persisted in considering incompatible. In this plate the floorboards, the bed, and the closet are all present. Everything concurs to give one the impression that the room's space is being shrunk, violently abridged under the onslaught of one of those nighttime fevers that warps vision—in this case, a vision perpetually irritated by the ambiguousness of things and the mystery of their hidden connections. The eye can hardly take in all the logical distortions resulting from an unbridled imagination strewing the scene with creatures and objects pertaining to antagonistic areas of reality, incompatible frames of reference. Yet the artist's genius renders these aberrations if not altogether believable at least plausible. The impact of this wooing of reason by the irrational is further enhanced by the collage technique. The choice of heterogeneous elements, their state and position (each retains its own proportions, its own vanishing point, its own speed, resistance, and original conditions), and, lastly, the skill with which the artist's hand disguises the breaks between different materials and antithetical sources: with these simple means Max Ernst, thanks to his magical touch, reinvents a universe of seemingly limitless hypnotic powers (e.g. *The Song of the Flesh*).

Marcel Duchamp
(1887-1968)
Monte Carlo Roulette Bond, 1924.
Photograph collage over printed matter.

NEGATORS, DESTROYERS, DISMANTLERS: GAME PLAYERS

For Duchamp, Man Ray, and Picabia pasted papers were never anything more than a means, one of several, to break with the art of the past; to reject an aesthetic sensibility that had prevailed for too long; and to replace it with the dry, simple rhythms of a visual mechanics. Collage substituted an impersonal procedure for the artist's all too human hand. It overturned century-old traditions of the Beautiful in art. It fostered the playful insolence of Picabia's work, the supreme nonchalance of Duchamp, and the ironic paradoxes of Man Ray. It enabled these three game players to develop a strategy of holding the eye in check for the mere pleasure of replaying the modest adventure of existence. This or that, here or there, today or tomorrow—what difference did it make?

All three artists concurrently adopted a scornful attitude towards painting in oils. As early as 1912, Duchamp, nauseated by the odour of turpentine, exchanged his brushes for "drier," cleaner techniques. To the thickness and fluidity of pigment he preferred the pencil's rigorousness, the fragile yet resistant transparency of glass, and, in time, the purely mental choice of the Readymade.

Francis Picabia mutinied against the clannishness of painters, their *artiste maudit* fantasies, their antiquated concern with *la petite sensation*, the telling little impression. He aimed his sarcasms at artists like Cézanne who spend their whole lives painting the same picture over and over again. Such was his scorn for academic art that he devised images with whatever lay at hand: buttons, toothpicks, matchsticks, and, in a supreme insult to purists, industrial enamel paints. As for Man Ray, his solitary experiments with the air brush between 1917 and 1919, his collages and stencillings, his subsequent interest in photography (it was easier to photograph a portrait than to paint one), and, lastly, his discovery of Rayographs, are all expressions of the same desire to "paint without a brush, canvas, or palette."

These three artists were considered by their peers to be destined for a brilliant future. Yet they abandoned the well-worn path that beckoned to them. Why? Doubtless the reason was precisely the failure of this future, which was undermined by the different aesthetic movements they had all participated in briefly —Impressionism, Fauvism, Cubism, Orphism—and with which they had all become disenchanted. This experience had convinced them that no single school's claim to render reality—any reality whatever —was acceptable. To them, art seemed to be cut off from life, a bone of contention between conflicting dogmas, a slave of a fatuous common "taste" and of the shortcomings of a society whose foundering idealisms, in a period of insouciance that was very soon to end in a carnage, were all too evident.

Each of them endeavoured in his own way to dismantle the machinery that lies behind common sense and the conventions of seeing. To the traditional ethic of honour, labour, and patriotism, they opposed a contrasting ethos of humour, indolence, and an aristocratic individualism. Blithely disregarding laws and conventions, they adopted a permanently contradictory, and self-contradictory, stance; they flaunted a gleeful amoralism, a flair for scandal, a magnificent nonchalance. Their lives were in tune with nothing except their own art, an art at once paradoxical, gratuitous, recondite, ephemeral, and useless.

In practice, this meant making a clean sweep of acquired knowledge and renewing the vocabulary and syntax of visual language. It meant drawing motifs from a wholly random repertory: a lampshade, a bicycle wheel, or a turbine was just as valid a subject as a conventional landscape, nude, or still life with fruit. Nor was this offhandedness limited to the choice of subject; it also extended to technique, which was reduced to a minimal gesture. To the disenchanted artists who had permanently renounced every illusion except that of their own pleasure, suspending an object from a string, laying it on the ground, or gluing it to a support was an effort-saving solution.

Yet this marked indifference towards the conventional elements in art, this casual surrender to the powers of the fortuitous and the possible, conceals beneath a mask of irony and dandyism an extraordinary degree of faith in the imagination. It amounted to what Duchamp called " a metaphysical assault on the irrational." To divert the viewer's attention away from the artist's hand is to permit the idea underpinning the art work to declare itself with greater clarity; it is to revert to a concept of painting as a *cosa mentale*, an intellectual adventure. It is also and above all a means of contributing, with the obscuring of the meaning which the artist simultaneously effects in the heart of each work, to the emergence of a "beauty of indifference" that affirms itself independently of any rational or intentional process: a neutral, absolute beauty that burns itself out in the irruption of the pure present. It is a philosophy suited to the desire for effacement which each of these three exceptional artists expressed at one point or another in his life: "We ought to secrete a special eraser fluid to blot out our works and their memory as we create them" (Picabia). All three had the same preoccupation with transparency, with an art that leaves no trail, akin to a decisive gambit on a chess board, an art where reality is redeemed by the trivial act of a taciturn artist covering his own tracks. If the Dadaism of Duchamp, Picabia, and Man Ray seems negative, it is so only in the Taoist sense: "The sage's way is to act without striving."

Here is a lamp, such as you might find in an early twentieth century manufacturer's catalogue or in a vignette accompanying a dictionary definition. Reduced to the flat, dimensionless, unshaded treatment of a blueprint, the image is as impermeable to any psychological interpretation as it is to any aesthetic intention. The meagre visual information consists, on one hand, of the blue line delineating the object and the unserviceable black cord curling around the lamp like an emblematic initial; and, on the other, of three pasted papers, almost devoid of meaning, bearing the artist's "signature" and two enigmatic statements in solemn typographical characters: *VOILÀ HAVILAND/LA POÉSIE EST COMME LUI/F. Picabia 1915 New York.*
It is impossible to be more cut-and-dry, more direct. The image has been pruned down to its barest essentials; it expresses no emotion, there is nothing to slow its legibility. This is poetry, an overwhelming revelation of an unmodified ordinary manufactured object, an assertion of reality reduced to its simplest expression. Yet, oddly enough, the more clearly inscribed is the object's profile the more removed it seems from the model it claims to reproduce. With the emergence of an absolute immediacy meaning withdraws; it drains into the vacuum of an excessive resemblance. Images that are as perfectly legible as this tend to drift. They seem to be expressing something else, like the Vanitas pictures of the seventeenth century. This effect of visual dizziness is amplified by the elliptical inscriptions Picabia has so cunningly added to the drawing. A little research reveals the fact that not only do the mysterious words designate Paul Haviland, a friend of the artist and the co-editor (with Alfred Stieglitz, who is the subject of a similar portrait)

of *291*, the New York review which first published Picabia's collage; but also the wording of these curious statements is in fact simply a parodistic allusion to stock phrases in the Larousse dictionary's Latin glossary: "Behold the man" (*Ecce Homo*) and "Poetry is like painting" (*Ut pictura poesis*). To the complete superficiality of the drawing and the triviality of the technical gesture is added the absurd mechanical reflex of a schoolboy dazed by rote learning parroting foreign phrases.

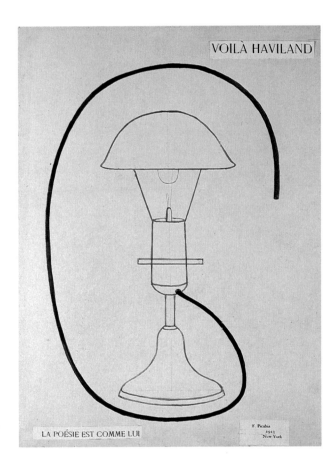

Francis Picabia
(1879-1953)
Behold Haviland/Poetry is Like Him, 1915.
Tempera and pasted paper.

Picabia's irony serves simultaneously to break up and revitalize a dead language.
Marcel Duchamp's invention of the Readymade is the ultimate expression of the will to destabilize clichés, whether visual or verbal, social or aesthetic, by sapping them through a variety of techniques including collage (which draws its efficacy from paradoxes, breaks in continuity, travesties, unmaskings, etc.). In lieu of the plastic values inherent to the art work and more especially to its material production, the Readymade substitutes the wholly abstract authority of a redemption through the mind, a pictorial nominalism

Man Ray
(1890-1976)
Dragonfly, 1916-1917.
From the *Revolving Doors* series.
Pasted paper.

that restores to the eye the child's spontaneous, gratuitous faculty of creation. Duchamp's declared purpose in creating *Monte Carlo Roulette Bond* (page 80) was to bankrupt the principality of Monaco's bank. Behind this boutade (and joking is always an essential part of Duchamp's strategy) looms a passion—perhaps this remarkable man's only passion—for games of chance. What fascinated him was not the emotional suspense of gambling or the hope of winning, but the field of random possibilities opened by the infinite combination of chess or the limitless permutations of martingales. The beauty (precisely a "beauty of indifference") of the endlessly renewed destruction of these permutations and combinations was enhanced by the repeated failures and fresh beginnings of what was to the artist a supreme metaphor for existence. The maquette of *Monte Carlo Roulette Bond* (which was destined to be reproduced in fifty copies) consists of a faithful reproduction of an official bond certificate overprinted on a halftone that repeats one of the puns Duchamp was so fond of: *moustiques domestiques demistock*. Over this first assemblage is superimposed a photograph (by Duchamp's friend Man Ray) of the artist transformed, with the help of a generous amount of shaving cream, into a Mephistophelian figure. This portrait is placed in the medallion normally reserved for the establishment's emblem. Lastly, the artist's signature and that of his female alias, Rose Sélavy (*c'est la vie*, another play on words), complete this brilliant display of non-sense that aims to subvert every certainty except the pleasure of laughing, living, and playing games of chance. From Monte Carlo where he had gone to try out his system, Duchamp wrote to Picabia: "It is deliciously monotonous. Not the slightest emotion. As you can see, I haven't stopped being a painter: now I'm drawing on chance."

Linked to Duchamp by a lifelong convergence of sensibilities, a companion on many of his escapades and his partner in the endless games of chess of which neither artist ever tired, Man Ray shared with his friend (as well as with Picabia) a mind receptive to chance and its propositions. The American artist's quest for pleasure was equalled only by his thirst for freedom. And this twofold need drove him to create bizarre objects that challenged preconceived ideas with no apparent exertion. In spite of his truly exceptional, universally recognized manual dexterity, Man Ray invariably gives one the impression that his creations were tossed off effortlessly. The only effort you see in his work is the effort to erase any traces of effort. And when his unflagging curiosity and inexhaustible inventiveness encounter an unforeseen obstacle, are diverted by a subconscious prompting, or discover a new and unexpected line of inquiry, he is able to turn these accidents to his advantage by viewing their occurrence as the driving force of artistic creation and the very substance of its activity.

In the series of ten collages entitled *Revolving Doors*, the appearance of pasted papers is thus less a reflection of a specific intention than a surrender to a greater degree of facility. It is the signature of an indolent detachment towards the work which is left to unfold its space independently of its creator; while the latter's role is reduced to that of influencing the conditions of a transcendent game being played outside himself.

El Lissitzky
(1890-1941)
Proun, 1923.
Lithograph and collage.

IN SEARCH OF THE FOURTH DIMENSION

NOTHING could be more clear-cut and resistant to the fluctuations of chance, it seems at first glance, than one of El Lissitzky's or Moholy-Nagy's compositions. A few simple shapes—circles, triangles, parallelograms—delimited by crisp contours and sparingly filled with pure, flat, ungradated colours articulate an exacting meditation on plastic signs. Forms and colours are reduced to the "zero level" of expressivity and the image is sustained solely by the endlessly diverse and subtle relationships between them. Yet as soon as you look more closely at one of these airy, ethereal constructions you feel that it would be impossible to be more indefinite. The composition has no centre, no firm connections with the edges. It floats aimlessly between depth and surface, top and bottom, front and back. The instant your eye settles on what appears to be something solid, the image you supposed was a kind of blueprint opens up and a multitude of alternative approaches immediately suggest themselves. Several potential perspectives seem to be juxtaposed and this dissolves the construction's apparent choicelessness and sets it adrift in an indefinite space. The collage's extra-pictorial materials may thus be drawn, in a wholly unpremeditated way, into the orbit of one of these small randomly floating systems. Their extraneous texture and the fact that, almost unconsciously, they bring into play the minimally disturbing functions of cutting out, assembling, and pasting (which generate attractions and repulsions and vibrant tensions between the elements) increase the multidimensional nature of the pictorial space created by bending the laws of Euclidean geometry. This is striking in Lissitzky's work. In his ample series of *Proun* compositions, for example, the combination of several visual axes within the same image (frontal, planimetric, lateral, uptilted, and down-tilted views) plunges the eye into a shifting network of conflicting possibilities. Counteracting the stability of the basic formal entities, the non-determination of the planes produced by these encounters and the simultaneousness of the directional references on the pictorial surface make the forms weightless and expand the pictorial space to infinity.

In Moholy-Nagy's pasted papers, on the other hand, the temporal factor is suggested by coloured elements organized in strata or else interwoven and repeated

—almost echoed—in registers of varied tonalities and proportions. Each visual entity carves space like a musical note rhythming time. The chromatic counterpoint and the relations between the forms which the Hungarian artist handles with an inexhaustible and consummately skilful inventiveness produce an impression of transparence, an extra visual dimension. This is an unprecedented enterprise, an attempt to give visual expression to the nonobservable data of the universe's unimaginably fast acceleration and expansion (which became a conceptual reality with the publication of Albert Einstein's theory of relativity).

The crisis of figuration that beset European painting from 1915 onwards, from Malevich's Suprematism to the Russian and Hungarian Constructivists, from Dada to Dutch Neo-Plasticism, reflected a need to wrest the work of art and the process of its coming into being from the grip of human time. Proclaiming *Victory Over the Sun*, as Kruchenykh did in 1913, and systematically rejecting the past as well as the future, as the adepts of Dada were doing all over Europe, involved more than just creating scandals and revolting against institutions. It was a way of summoning a new order to replace the heliocentric order that had dominated for centuries: a brighter metaphysical universe swept by an ampler spirit, a universe whose signs and boundless space required new expressive tools. The iconoclasms variously manifested by the "anti-art" paradox of Dada and the pure abstraction of painters like Mondrian, Van Doesburg, and Kandinsky thus appear as expressions (and they are analogous expressions) of a desire to avoid the pitfalls of historicism and the repetitions which the recent avant-gardes had fallen into one after the other. This attempt to move beyond earlier practices and assumptions, this desire to purify the creative act by ridding it of the complaisances that surround it and of the preconceived ideas that enshrine it, explains Duchamp's Readymades and Picabia's ephemeral pictures as well as the Constructivists' weightless translucent compositions. All these painters shared the same dream of a virgin age tinged with "either nostalgia" or hope. They dreamt of a paradise that could be regained by abandoning figurative representation. They wanted to relegate the dramaturgy of the human lot, with all its contingencies, to reaches that were light-years distant; they wanted to dissolve it in a nameless expanse. And they wanted to replace personal decisions, discipline, and the whole gamut of virtues commonly associated with artistic genius by unpredictable decisions, tokens of freedom and openness, and a supreme Randomness that would engender a suprarational objectivity.

Under the impact of this radical questioning of the logical guideposts which shape our perceptions and understanding of art works, the eye's scope was increased. Its ability to see from afar was enhanced, albeit to the detriment of participating in the warmth of beings and the immediacy of simple things. From now on all that mattered to the De Stijl theorists, the Constructivists, and the painters pooling their experimental work at the Bauhaus, were networks of lines of force, points of tension, and new equilibriums invisibly produced by colliding particles of plastic energy crossing the pictorial field. Not only did the themes of easel painting lose ground to the magnified, exclusive structures of pure composition; not only were the specific lights which rhythm the day in traditional painting deprived of their shadows (those mortal premonitions with which our earthly lot is identified) and absorbed in interacting relative velocities and asymmetrical rhythms; not only were they dissolved in the instantaneousness of all moments captured, thanks to the multiplication of viewpoints, in a single flash. But even more vitally perhaps, the specific properties of two-dimensional painting were extended to other less strictly speculative modes of visual expression, like the graphic arts, furniture design, environmental design, sculpture, and, most of all, architecture.

Indeed the stunning architectural creations of this period are brilliant embodiments of the plastic artists' aspirations towards weightlessness and transparency. With their broken asymmetrical volumes thrusting skywards, those steel and glass constructions appear to defy the law of gravity and to flout the authority of monocular vision.

In forging a language capable of translating the complexity and mobility of that new optical reality, collage offered an additional means of depersonalizing the image. It enabled the artist to eliminate the human residue in painting. It helped him to get rid of whatever was extraneous to the real nature of painting and to protect the work of art from the irrelevant drama taking place inside the painter. The cutout's mechanical directness reinforced the neutrality of the plastic sign. It gave more emphasis to forms and made for a clearer perception of coloured planes. Depending on its intensity, size, outline, and position within the com-

Willi Baumeister
(1889-1955)
Chess Players, 1923.
Pen and ink, gouache, crayons, collage.

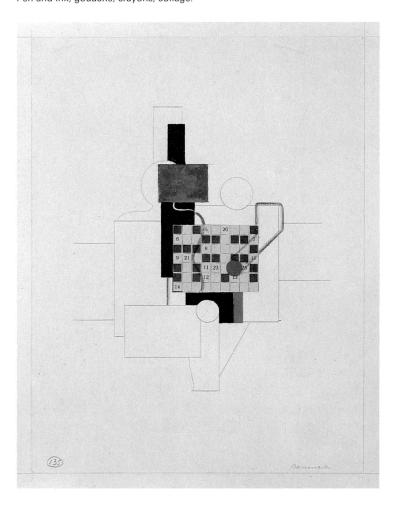

Laszlo Moholy-Nagy
(1895-1946)
Collage with Black Centre, 1922.
Collage.

position, each fragment generated a pull of attraction, a gravitational field, a pulsation of energies that recalls the hidden forces governing the heavenly bodies in interstellar space. Finally, the restrained gesture whereby the discernible trace of the brush was replaced by the undifferentiated manipulations of collage situated the artist's presence somewhere between the intentional and the arbitrary: a strange non-intervention which expressed the self's fusion with the autonomous space of the work.

And so, to conclude, one might say that the discreteness of the collaged element's physical presence on the surface of this type of image gives the alien fragment a potential for serenity that is inversely proportional to the power—and it is a disturbing power—of the newspaper cutting or painted paper in a Cubist composition. Instead of leading the eye back to the data of external reality, instead of impressing it with the immediate rough texture of the tangible world, it allows it to become detached. It dematerializes any breaks in visual continuity and places the eye in a state of suspended restfulness akin to certain oriental states of repose wherein organic rhythms which elude rational thought are perceived to unfold in silence.

Max Ernst
(1891-1976)
Loplop Introduces, c. 1931.
Pencil and collage.

MIDWAY BETWEEN DREAMING AND REALITY

WHEN André Breton invited Max Ernst to exhibit his collages in May-June 1921 at Au Sans Pareil, a bookshop on the Avenue Kléber in Paris, this was to influence both the life of the German artist (who settled in Paris a year later) and the birth of Surrealism itself. Surrealism was not yet an independent movement, but the young French poets grouped around the review *Littérature* had held aloof on several occasions from the "great negative task" advocated by those impeccable and indomitable Dadaists, Tristan Tzara and Francis Picabia. During those same months when Ernst was exhibiting his works (under the title *Mise Sous Whisky Marin*, which might be translated "Sealed Under Marine Whiskey") the small group of Parisian Surrealists, soon joined by Robert Desnos, Paul Eluard, René Crevel, and others, were experimenting with various techniques of psychic liberation: exploring the fringes of sleep, probing the mysteries of the subconscious, provoking controlled abnormal mental states in order to find new images and richer correlations between things. These youthful survivors of the barbarity of World War One were filled with contempt for the petty values and apathy of a society that was caught, they felt, in the rut of banality. They wanted to explore areas of the mind that had never been charted. They were ready to employ almost any means to split open the hard shell of rational thought and tap the vital, precious veins of deeper meaning where man's being, freed from inhibition and prejudice, can quench its thirst for the marvellous and discover new, wider horizons.

The collages Max Ernst sent to Paris struck these artists and writers with all the force of a genuine revelation. Twenty years later, in his *Genèse et perspective artistiques du Surréalisme*, Breton was still under their spell: "I remember the excitement, the likes of which we were never to experience again, that filled us, Tzara, Aragon, Soupault, and myself, when we saw them for the first time. The outer object had broken away from its usual context, its elements had so to speak emancipated themselves, so that they entered into entirely new relations with one another, thus escaping the reality principle even though they remained substantial on the level of reality." The tremendous power of displacement which Breton recognized at once in Ernst's small visual constructions was a perfect example, he felt, of the poetics of surprise which he himself was elaborating at the time. The principle on which this poetics rested lay in bringing two distant realities together so as to produce a rich and electrifying "surreality" possessing a beauty and power sparked by "the difference in potential between the two conductors." In the optical manipulations suggested by the painter's restless imagination, the poet discerned an obvious kinship with the results of automatic writing which he and Philippe Soupault had recorded in *Les Champs magnétiques*. In both cases the stale signs of ordinary reality were charged with a disquieting force. With a splendid imperviousness to reason, the same spontaneity condensed dream-figures in both, projections of desire and lost memory; the same absurdities, the same unexpected conjunctions revealed themselves to be meaningful in both and in both they had the same function: to uproot the reader or viewer from his familiar context and transport him to an inner territory where no form of rational censorship exists. To all who undertook it, this adventure brought an extraordinary weightlessness, an unparalleled degree of freedom.

Now, both collage and automatic writing required a special sensitivity as well as capacity to let go yet, at the same time, remain in control. The Surrealist artist or writer who wanted to "photograph" thought itself —in other words, capture its flow and sudden illuminations—had to place himself in a state of vigilant passivity, a drowsy awareness which was nevertheless permeable to the raw data supplied by the conscious part of his mind. Only then could the promptings of his inner being come to the surface, startling crystallizations that either occurred randomly or were elaborated by the intellect. Denying himself the romantic privilege of creating a coherent whole from nothing, Ernst viewed himself less as an artist in the traditional sense than as a mediator between the imagination and nature. Because he questioned everything and set no limits to his curiosity, he felt that his task was simply to connect spaces that are usually held to be incompatible. This insistence on maintaining lines of communication between objective reality and the reality of the imagination, between the daytime and the nocturnal realms; this determination to combine the magic of the macrocosm with the en-

Défais ton sac, mon brave.

Plus légère que l'atmosphère, puissante et isolée : Perturbation, ma sœur, la femme 100 têtes.

Max Ernst
(1891-1976)
Two illustrations for *La Femme 100 Têtes*, 1929.
Collage.

chantments of the microcosm, the spell of appearances with the fascinating hidden side of things, forced him paradoxically to be very exacting about the materials he selected and the ways he combined them to create his astonishing images.

Indeed, contrary to what you would expect, nothing arbitrary or facile can be found at this stage of Ernst's work. Rather you notice an intensification of his faculties of perception and imagination, a greater methodicalness, a vibrant contraction of his eye as he searches for a flaw in appearances that will permit him to slip from one order of reality to another, an irritating detail that will suggest unheard of analogies and associations. There are strict criteria governing his borrowings from manufacturers' catalogues, scientific manuals, and illustrated novels. His images are never superficially connected, his associations are never vulgar.

And formidable as the semantic displacement in his collages may seem at times, they nonetheless have a formal coherence that resists the pull of anarchy with its own logic. Werner Spies's recent work on Ernst's collages reveals how fastidiously the artist strove to give his images a plausible reading, how careful he was to respect not only the proportions of the figures he included in his compositions but also the intervals between the chisel and gouge marks in the woodblock illustrations he combined, the colours of the pieces of paper he pasted together, and even the

"style" of the engravings he pirated. By cutting out and adjusting the fragments, he was able to bring out graphic tensions lacking in the original engravings. Yet he sought to disguise obvious physical breaks and seams (unlike the Cubist *collagistes* and Dada photomontage artists who emphasize the atomization of the elements that make up the image). And in fact the seams are invisible in the printed reproductions of Ernst's published collages.

Now the fact that the artist's handiwork is concealed and the lines of juncture between the elements in his collages are masked by a clever use of trompe-l'oeil serves mainly to create an effect of surprise. It helps to shift the viewer's attention from the mechanics of image-making to the image's contents. The art of Ernst's collages—especially those extraordinary private dramas, *La Femme 100 Têtes* and *Une Semaine de Bonté*—is akin to that of a magician pulling rabbits out of a hat. By shifting visual meanings in a way that seems so natural it goes unnoticed, the artist is able to give a new meaning to the fragments of reality he combines in his works. A master of illusionism, he perhaps used this procedure to settle scores with the pictorial realism of his father's generation (a school of painting that had no qualms about modifying nature to adapt it to the requirements of picture-making). At any event, collage becomes a kind of alchemistry in Ernst's hands: it connects man to the products of his imagination, yet respects the essence

Max Ernst
(1891-1976)
Illustration for *Une Semaine de Bonté*, 1934.
From Part Two, "L'Eau "
Collage.

of both. By playing on equivalences and affinities Ernst is able to enrich the phenomenal world with innumerable internal postulates suggested by his boundless curiosity. An act of hallucinatory transmutation carried out in the artist's hypersensitized mind (or *mutatis mutandis* in that of any poet or dreamer), requiring only his medium's receptivity to bring its inflorescences to the surface, the collage process does not really need glue at all. Ernst's humorous maxim in reply to an acquaintance who asked him what sort of glue he was using—"If it is not plumes that make plumage, it is not glue (*colle*) that makes collage"— shows that in his view technique was subordinate to the visionary powers of the artist who bends it to his own needs.

All this suggests that we should perhaps view Ernst's entire oeuvre from the standpoint of collage. No other concept offers a better definition of the paintings the artist executed between 1922 and 1929. In these works the brush has the same function as the collage process whereby "two apparently incompatible realities meet on a plane that seems foreign to both. ' By creating an illusion of collage without actually employing pasted papers the painter brilliantly demonstrates the metatechnical validity of the collage procedure.

Frottage (rubbing), which Ernst discovered in 1925 while contemplating some floorboards (in a situation of isolation and sensorial irritability identical to that which had led him to adopt collage six years earlier), can likewise be reduced to a purely inner model. Despite the difference between these two procedures, both produced an intensification of his visionary powers. Ernst used them interchangeably: they both served as stimulants and supports for his creative visions. Like other techniques which his ever vigilant imagination devised later (dripping, decalcomanias, scraping), collage and frottage were means that allowed him to witness the birth of a work of art as a virtual onlooker. They helped him to go "beyond painting" to a state where he himself was both subject and agent of the image. An androgynous observer of his own diverseness, his own contradictoriness, his own evasions, his own obsessions, he could thus set down on paper "that which made itself seen within" himself.

Ernst's images oscillate between two worlds. They teeter on the borderline between reality and the imagination, objective phenomena and subjective impulses, facts and the whisperings of memory and desire. This is why they impress your retina with a feeling that you are already familiar with their strange geography. You have already experienced the events they depict, though you cannot identify them positively. As in dreams or in moments of hypnagogical drowsiness when phrases and images swirl around and combine without any order in your freely ranging mind, you feel that meaning is knocking on the windowpane. It is on the tip of your tongue, yet it eludes you. It seems so near, yet is so far. Caught in this predicament, your eye is forced to become more agile: it learns to break up appearances, jumble them, and even invert them. You experience the relativity of the visible (which is the eye's special field). You discover its propensity to change into its opposite at any moment and to reverse logical relations, whether temporal or spatial. Having reached this stage, your eye can now slip through the looking-glass and venture at its own risk to push back the limits of knowledge.

Ernst's ambition was to rescue his fellow creatures from blindness. Like Rimbaud half a century before him he carried out his visionary program by "slowly putting all his senses out of kilter" and radically questioning the tools and practices associated with making art works. He practised this method with such diligence that he was eventually able to claim: "I too have turned myself into a visionary." Using collage's potential for "putting things out of kilter," Ernst, the "blind swimmer" (as he called himself), the artist intimately acquainted with dark forests and nocturnal cruelties, succeeded in transcending the frontiers, conventions, timetables, and habits that divide genders and nations and ways of seeing.

THE friendship that sprang up between Paul Eluard and Max Ernst at their first meeting soon produced (in 1922) two books of combined poetry and collage: *Répétitions* and *Les Malheurs des Immortels*. They contain Ernst's favourite themes—ornithology, sadistic eroticism, mutilated bodies, ubiquitous gesticulating hands, wounded eyes—and, on page after page, they reveal the deft conjurer's touch of an artist who wanted above all to enchant and astonish his audience. The cover vignette of *Répétitions*, for example, could be a manifesto of the art of collage according to Ernst. The mysteriously multiplied hands seem to have been set in motion solely by their own desire to irritate the viewer's eye or subject it to a savage surgery—and the surgical theme is a dominant one of Surrealist art—in order to expose it to more distant vistas and increase its resistance to sudden surges of poetic intensity.

Starting with material that has no aesthetic value, the artist amazes us with his infinitely delicate and cruel tricks. He turns meanings inside out like gloves; and so fascinating are the non-sequiturs and lacunae of the fragments he juggles that you want to "get a closer look" at them, you want to peek at the secrets of the conjurer manipulating the invisible threads of mean-

ing. An Ernst collage is an invitation to daydream as well as to muse on the modality of the image's emergence and the conditions that determine the way it functions.

IN this second collage from *Répétitions*, Ernst makes the initial material undergo such a subtle transformation that the model (the *Eve* from Dürer's 1504 print) cannot be recognized. Yet the process of semantic disruption rests on such minute formal dislocations, such fastidious alterations, that in spite of being disconcerted the eye is able to cling to familiar contours. For example, the anatomy on the left is broken up, yet the permutated elements are arranged with a certain symmetry. The graft on the leg is executed so perfectly that it almost seems natural. The impact of the frighteningly disproportionate birds is softened by the fact that they have the same shape and are the same size. Even the brutal decapitation of the woman seems less than definitive. Through a series of signs ranging from top to bottom, outside to inside, small to large shapes, the missing head's function is transferred to an enormous inverted shell, thus giving birth to this modern Venus bred by the artist's tormented imagination.

Max Ernst
(1891-1976)
Cover for Paul Eluard's
Répétitions, 1922.
Collage.

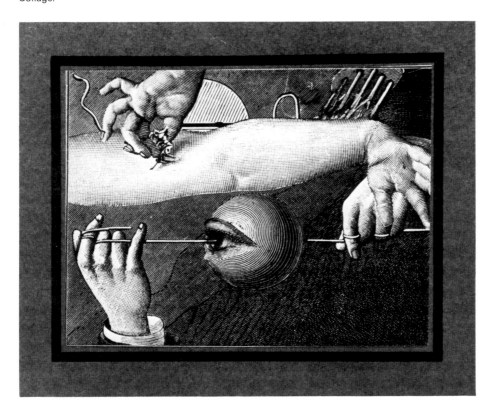

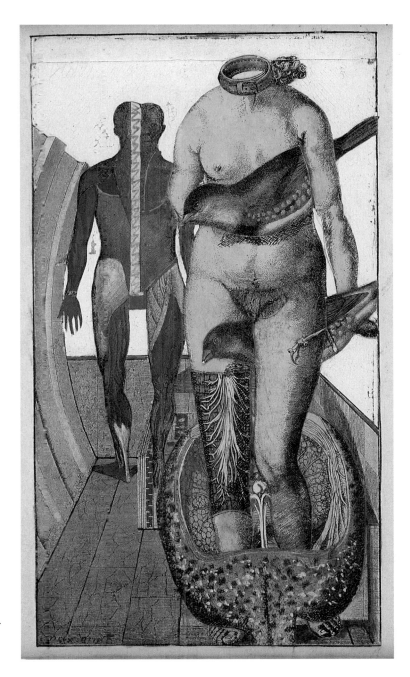

Max Ernst
(1891-1976)
Speech or Bird-Woman, 1921.
Illustration for Paul Eluard's
Répétitions.
Collage and gouache.

ALTHOUGH Ernst used collage mainly to produce an effect of *dépaysement*—exile in a strange setting—he was nevertheless always careful to give the bizarre scenes he created a reassuringly familiar, almost nti- mate air. The tension between his absurd visual propositions and the obviously domestic space which encloses them produces a curious perceptual disor- der: the viewer loses his bearings and begins to float. Indeed, a feeling of weightlessness pervades Ernst's work. It is manifested by such actions as falling, leaping into thin air, flying, swimming, drifting into somnolence, having an ecstatic convulsion. Wings, feathers, fins, wind filled skirts, and oscillating spheres express a leaden ease of movement that re- calls the sluggishness of certain dreams. The main emblematic figure in Ernst's private menagerie of am- phibious creatures, vampires, ectoplasms, and mer- maids driven by invisible motors is the artist's Doppel- gänger Loplop, the Bird Superior, who flits across the border between the rational and the imaginary with the greatest of ease.

In the 1922 collage entitled *The Fall of an Angel* the triple figure's random plunge is relativized by the "frame by frame" breakdown of the moments that mark the different stages of her fall and by the jux- taposition of logically incompatible spatial realities (a juxtaposition which incidentally reflects the procedure's arbitrary supremacy). Collage permits the artist to do away with the logical reference points that would ordinarily solicit your eye. Ernst thus succeeds in transporting you to another dimension—almost a supplementary dimension—where the figure appears and disappears like an obsessive, falsely familiar im- age (*falsely familiar* because the striped wallpaper's meaning has been subverted), an angel that, if you look at the figure closely, is no angel at all. There is something diabolical about Ernst's illusionist witch- craft here. Flouting his own method, he uses a brush to define the triple figure sharply and crisply, painting a false shadow to outline her against the unified field of the decorative background. Adding a dizzying semantic twist to a dizzying technical twist in what amounts to a double involution within the work, Ernst creates an illusion of collage with paint and thereby announces a host of paintings which, from this date until he again began to produce illustrated novels, illustrate the essentials of the collage procedure with- out employing glue.

Max Ernst
(1891-1976)
Illustration for *Une Semaine de Bonté*, 1934.
From Part Five, "La Clé des Chants."
Collage.

IN 1929 Ernst took up collage illustrations again, producing three works in rapid succession. The most famous, *La Femme 100 Têtes* (The Hundred Headless Woman), contains some 150 plates. In contrast to the earlier books done with Eluard, where each poem carries its own separate explosive charge with no attempt at continuity, the principle of displacement is systematically applied to the narrative content in the collage novels. They are divided into chapters or days of the week; they have recurring themes and their migrant heroes counterfeit a fragile albeit plausible existential density and duration, one rendered more tenuous still by the breaks in the collages and the hiatuses in the printed text itself. In these interstitial spaces unrelated memories condense, hybrid figures flit past and reappear unexpectedly. The elemental forces of nature saturate these scenes with their disproportionately extended or shortened perspectives where ordinary objects, duplicated almost *ad nauseam*, evoke the tangled, infinitely elastic fabric of dreams. Fascinated from youth by Freud's research on the dream process, Ernst viewed the narrative development of images as a technique for illustrating the discursive essence of dreams (though, unlike Freud,

he avoided attempting any dream interpretation). Resisting all impulses to explain the dream content of his work, he concentrated exclusively on visual material. From his vantage point on the threshold of the explicit he observed—a sometimes amused, sometimes anxious spectator—the inconclusive combinations that occur in dreams and he used collage to record those that were most suggestive and poetic on paper.

More than ever before, his appropriation of the collage technique required a totally banal background. Both on the aesthetic and the semantic level, the engravings the artist pirated to create the settings for his startling little dramas were deliberately neutral so as to give more potency, by force of contrast, to the figures and objects he then grafted onto them. The deadpan bourgeois interiors from nineteenth century illustrated popular novels, the topographic views of Paris, the street scenes, the historical tableaux: they are the iconographic foundations that sustain the obsessions of "the most magnificently haunted brain in existence today," to quote André Breton's splendid description of the artist in the "Note to the Reader" at the beginning of *The Hundred Headless Woman*.

Max Ernst
(1891-1976)
The Fall of an Angel, 1922.
Oil and collage.

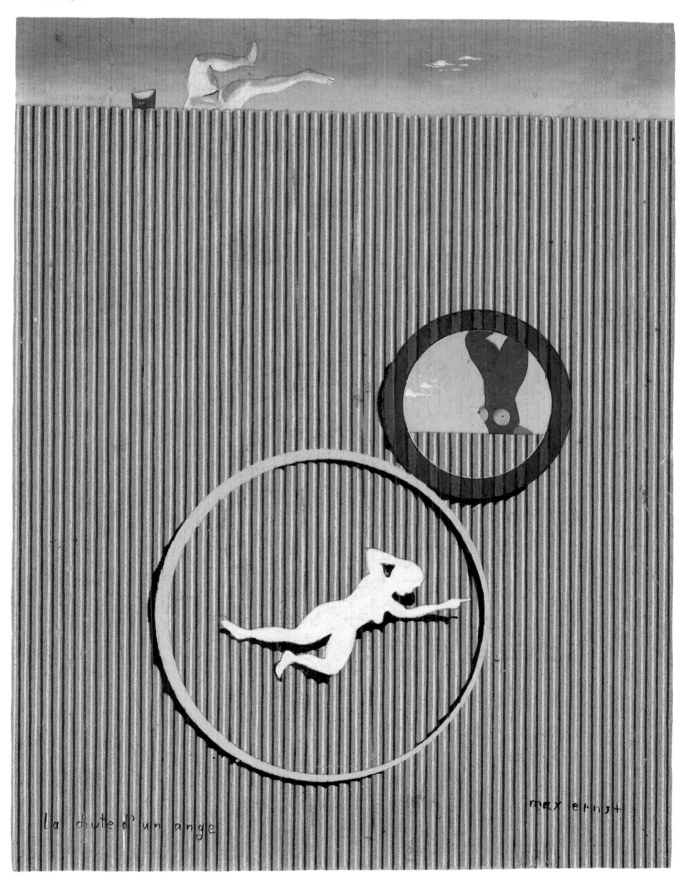

la chute d'un ange

max ernst

Max Ernst
(1891-1976)
Homage to a Little Girl Named Violette, 1933.
Pencil and collage.

IN the three collage novels, Ernst's mastery of the collage technique and his sensitivity to the suggestions inherent in the models he selects enable him to unlock the bizarre world inside him. With an unequalled inventiveness he employs scissors and glue (though he then eliminates any trace of them by having his original collages run off in "clean" typographical reproductions) to express a violence and erotic ambiguousness that were already discernible beneath a veneer of irony in his Cologne period. In the illustrated books, collage serves consistently to exclude, to banish, to threaten; it makes the most innocuous settings appear perilous; it changes kisses into vampires' suckings, quiet travellers into assassins. Not even the artist's couple of agitators, Loplop the Bird Superior and his sister Perturbation, the Hundred Headless Woman, are immune to the contagion of perversion which

runs through the 1929 novel. They never embrace; mutilated, dispossessed of their own selves, they are doomed to follow each other endlessly from one realm to another. They are driven by the insane hope of eventually fusing their mutually contradictory natures: a dream of an androgynous union that would abolish the restrictive conditions of classical dialectics and materialize the "convulsive identity" the artist advocates, an identity that would respect the complexity and diversity of being to a greater extent than anything we know.

YET these were also the years when Loplop the Bird Superior, the "third person painter," to use Werner Spies's ingenious expression, was viewing, with an amused glint in his eye, the birth of large pasted papers radically different from the clever vignettes of the collage novels. The bird-painter, who is always delineated in dry mechanical lines, gestures with arge simplified hands towards an image affixed to an easel formed by his own body: an engraved plate from an encyclopedia, a photograph, a printed notice, or, as shown here, a wrinkled scrap of paper which adds a palpable relief to the already arresting optical effect of the work.

What lesson, if any, does the clairvoyant bird mean to teach us during his brief sojourn on earth? What is the meaning of his insistence on displaying images always presenting them frontally, spreading them out with ostentation, using all the devices of pedantic

the visible functions and what is at stake when it comes into being. Painting is a mirror held up to itself. In a gesture that came to exclude all other gestures in the artist's remaining years, it begins to observe itself being made. By drawing our attention to the physical process of making a collage, by rendering it conspicuous, the magician in Ernst, overwhelmed by his own powers, deliberately breaks the spell of that mysterious coherence which has been the hallmark of his art up until now. Weary of playing the mystagogue, the sly ironic conjuror at last reveals the secrets of his art to his victims and allows them, though only for an instant, to accede freely to the occult mechanisms whereby images are formed.

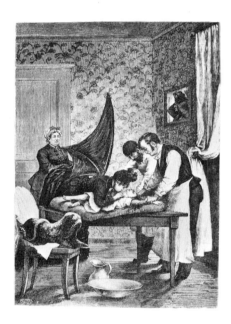

argumentation: fastidious draughtsmanship, a profusion of borders and frames, emphatically repeated signs? Why is the artist who up until now has disguised all traces of his magical manipulations suddenly so anxious to open our eyes to his conjuror's tricks? The witty self-portrait that Ernst elaborated between 1929 and 1934 in a series of collages entitled *Loplop Introduces* is said to be a distillation of the artist's sharp awareness of his own intellectual and creative powers. Depicting himself both as a creator and as a surface on which coolly objective images are projected, Ernst appears to be telling us that he is successively the author, subject, and critic of his own work. At the same time he is warning us not to try and reduce his art to a mere translation of reality (whatever the reality, whether it is obscure or objective, familiar or distant). Increasingly, it is a reflection on the way

Loplop, ivre de peur et de fureur, retrouve sa tête d'oiseau et reste immobile pendant 12 jours des deux côtés de la porte.

Max Ernst
(1891-1976)
Illustration for *Une Semaine de Bonté*, 1934.
From Part Three, "La Cour du Dragon."
Collage.

◁ Illustration for *La Femme 100 Têtes*, 1929.
Collage.

Joan Miró
(1893-1983)
Untitled, summer 1929.
Pasted paper, pastel, gouache, pencil.

BEYOND PAINTING

"Let's not forget that other conquest of collage: Surrealist painting," Max Ernst once quipped. Most historians of the Surrealist movement wou'd agree with the somewhat paradoxical statement that the principle underlying the distinctive fantasies of Surrealism stems from collage. André Breton himself was well aware of this connection: he declared in 1945 that "Surrealism benefited at once from the collages of 1920 which proposed a visual organization that was completely new yet corresponded to what Lautréamont and Rimbaud had wanted to do in poetry."

An allusion to those poetic forerunners of Surrealism, Lautréamont's *Les Chants de Maldoror* (1868-1869) and Rimbaud's *Les Illuminations* (1872-1873), appears as early as 1930 in a remarkable essay entitled "La Peinture au défi" ("The Challenge to Painting") which Aragon wrote to preface a collage exhibition at the Galerie Goemans in Paris. The first to discern the real scope of the new language invented by Max Ernst and to give a penetrating definition of it, Aragon makes the following critically important point: "Modern collage demands our attention for the way it combines things, in total contrast to painting, beyond painting." The concept of a plural, composite art that is forever extending and amending its own terms of definition was born. It was to have a tremendous growth during the ensuing decades.

The Surrealist artists, those new eclectics, cared little about what materials and methods they used as long as their art communicated a sense of magic. They viewed Beauty as an outmoded preconception, an antiquated privilege. They saw collage (not unlike dreaming itself) as an effective tool for prying open the gates of the unknown.

Moreover collage had one signal and inviting advantage: it required no training. It made no stylistic demands; it could even dispense with harmony and inspiration. It was a game that anyone could play, at any time. The adepts of collage liked to draw their models, materials, and moods from that rather silly, vaguely sentimental stock of images utterly lacking in any aesthetic value that had captivated Rimbaud and coloured his vocabulary: *idiotic pictures, overdoor decorations, jugglers' backcloths, street signs, cheap colour prints*, or their literary equivalent (which delighted the Surrealist poets Aragon, Breton, Eluard and, later, Jacques Prévert and Georges Hugnet), *antiquated writings, church Latin, poorly spelled erotic books, old-fashioned novels, fairy tales, children's books, fusty operas, simple-minded refrains, naive rhythms.*

The sympathy for popular art in its various guises (the trivial, the playful, the derisive) reflected the Surrealists' common desire to combat the arrogance of bourgeois institutions and the hierarchy of established dogmas. But mainly it testified to the Surrealist movement's unflaggingly generous curiosity about all those expressions of human sensitivity, including those that were banned, marginal, despised or forgotten, which promised to bring back to art a childish and gratuitous spirit, and indeed an enlivening appeal. Collage does not exclude any form of being, known and unknown. It is open spontaneously to the innumerable subconscious suggestions contained in the image. It seeks no answers and no triumphs other than surprise, the flash of a transient flame. In the hands of the Surrealists, those visual revolutionaries of the twenties and thirties, it was a perfect instrument for fusing the free, untamed, unconscious subject with the elusive, unpredictable, polymorphous oneness of the universe.

From the mid-twenties on, Max Ernst's seminal discoveries in the field of collage, which were soon commented on abundantly, aroused curiosity and interest wherever the Surrealist teachings took root: in Belgium, Britain, Czechoslovakia and, a little later, in the United States. Admirers of Ernst's art adopted his solutions, dreamed his dreams. Many of them followed in his footsteps, but none of them ever succeeded in reaching the same degree of poetic concentration, the same balance, maintained year in, year out, between the graphic tension of the image's components and the explosive force of a subliminal message that releases its energy, and at the same time discloses its enigma, in a convulsive upsurge.

Collage was used increasingly in Surrealist circles at the time we are speaking of (it seemed to offer the best, if not the only, means of attaining the state of permanent metaphor which the Surrealists all sought), but its effectiveness and capacity for plastic renewal were beginning to wane. For the success of Surrealism's visual strategy was hereafter to hinge less

René Magritte
(1898-1967)
Untitled, 1928.
Watercolour, collage and pencil.

on the formal qualities of each term engaged in the attack on conventional logic than on the electrifying difference between their semantic charges. Consequently, the stages of the elaboration of Surrealist images were skipped more and more often, and the physical manipulations underlying the image were now often concealed.

Compared to the classical mechanics of the pasted paper where each break is shown clearly, each logical relation spelled out, and each disparity explainable, the elliptical style of the "visionary" Surrealist artists seemed to exist in a more fluid, apparently expanding space. The phenomena condensed within this space result from causes, movements, and velocities which are rendered extremely improbable by the non-representational character of the decisions that order them.

Released from the limitations of a purely technical procedure which had thus far confined the pasted paper to the register of painting, collage was now free to spread its tentacular imagination in all directions irrespective of genres and quantities. Its inexhaustible combinations were now found in photography and in the cinema. They were prominent where the artist's touch was invisible: in Dali's phantasmal deliriums, in Brauner's disquieting forays into the heart of the enigma that tormented him. At times their associative freedom obeyed the laws of spontaneity and chance, at other times it was governed by the unconscious. In Miró's bizarre assemblages, in Joseph Cornell's boxes, in Meret Oppenheim's provocatively sensual trick objects it produced laughter, surprise, anxiety, even gasps.

Again, the ability to switch the signs of the outer world (by means of the interpenetrations, permutations, and transparencies that are possible in a purely mental space where objects, untrammelled by any obstacles, are able to move about freely) produces the erotic "perversions" which Bellmer's dolls engage in in their passionate striving for unity. Finally, we owe to the diabolical ingenuity of the Surrealist imagination those strictly speculative pleasures offered by the visual conundrums which Man Ray and René Magritte began to devise in the 1920s.

Initially conceived as an instrument to bring the visible to act on the viewer, a "new machine for seeing," as it was called in the heyday of Cubism, collage, thanks to a shift in function that is unprecedented in art history, developed into a machine for reflecting about the act of seeing. It became the tool of a formidable intelligence which turned the art work into a field of invention and discovery where the not yet invalidated conditions for a language of art can be questioned with increasing accuracy. With its draughtsman's instruments (rulers, squares, compasses, and curve-tracers) embedded in liberal applications of glue, Man Ray's 1935 assemblage entitled *Collage ou l'Age de la colle* ("Collage or the Age of Glue") is a perfect example of this shifting aesthetic: the medium, which had hitherto served to articulate the image's content, is now the actual theme of the work.

Under the impact of the Surrealist poets' subversive efforts to destabilize signs, the contamination of the image by discourse about the image, which Marcel Duchamp had initiated in 1913, characterized the Surrealist enterprise from beginning to end. This is why the Surrealist collage, which stems directly from Lautréamont's famous "encounter between a sewing machine and an umbrella on a dissecting table," usually seems to be the result of an abstract metaphoric process that subordinates formal intentions to a kind of poetic explosion. Scissors and glue were no longer necessary: the heterogeneousness of the combined fragments was sufficient to make their encounter significant. The pre-eminence of the idea over plastic considerations or contingencies lent legitimacy to the indiscriminate use of diverse, unexpected materials, daring techniques of assemblage, and arresting composite images (*cadavres exquis*, object poems, object dreams, as they were termed) which the Surrealists devised in their attempts to extend the boundaries of painting. But on the other hand, painting's annexation of the purely mental character of poetic discourse (stylistic figures creating diversions in the intangible space of words) helped to render the simple pleasures of seeing, the passive, ecstatic enjoyment of contemplating a work of art, significantly less important than the satisfaction of the intellect relishing the mastery of semiotics.

René Magritte's painting is an exemplary product of the aristocratic disenchantment cultivated by the Surrealists. It conceals technical gestures behind cunning trompe-l'oeil; it has a misleading appearance of academic craftsmanship, but in fact it consists of elaborate visual traps which trip up the image and its signifier, the word and its referent. In his bogus collages (dismal scenes which open on bleak, vacant glimpses behind the stage, theatrical groupings of objects which seem about to be joined in sterile nuptials), this

fierce grammarian of nonsense appears to be inventing a new physics where signs change locations, reverse their charges without the ghost of a warning, simultaneously affirm and deny their relations with other signs.

Magritte's collages propose an endless and disconcerting variety of hypothetical situations; they create an indeterminacy that is at times inspiring, at other times disappointing. Thus day and night cancel each other in an atmosphere of complete indifference in the *Empire of Lights*; in *La Clef des Champs*, a shattered window pane declares the tautology of inside and outside and refutes every possibility of escape; finally, the legend of *Ceci n'est pas une pipe* ("This is not a pipe") tells us that every reality becomes suspect the moment it is articulated by a code. There is something uncanny about the convergence and indeed

René Magritte
(1898-1967)
La Clef des Champs, 1933.
Oil on canvas.

coincidence between Magritte's subtle visual equations and the findings of contemporary (1923-1926) quantum physics. Like Magritte's pictures the three main principles of quantum physics (indeterminacy, complementarity, and non-location) describe a chaotic, random reality indescribably and unpredictably in motion which is altered by the act of observation (incidentally, one can compare Duchamp's "onlooker" to the observer in modern physics).

In contrast to this intellectual defence where painting, because it attempts to demonstrate too much, often loses a great deal of that which makes it beautiful, the technique of the pasted paper, somewhat neglected in the wake of Max Ernst's successes with collage, came back in favour with certain artists who were temperamentally removed from the interminable theoretical discussions and power struggles besetting the Surrealist movement. Artists like Arp, Miró, and Picasso rarely experimented with this rediscovered technique in large-scale works, or in works which they intended to finish, but they used it to try out new plastic solutions, investigate new materials, search for new resonances.

Born in the privacy of the artist's studio, spawned by intuition or elaborated by trial and error in moments of discouragement when colours and arabesques seemed to have lost their brilliance—or perhaps merely dashed off in moments of relaxation from the pressures of creation—these rough sketches, projects, and experiments contain the first stirrings of creation. They speak of the violence of the initial creative upsurge, the buzzing of elementary forces struggling into existence, the artist's urge to express himself, his anxieties and obsessions. They are fragile, unpolished, unspectacular. One feels that there is something almost indecent about looking at them. Yet it was thanks to the freedom of their forms and textures, the unintended effects obtained by cutting and gluing, the haste or clumsiness with which they were assembled, that Arp, Miró, and Picasso, almost without realizing what they were doing, often put the finger on something fundamental about the nature of the artistic vision. Thanks to these private assemblages they succeeded now and then in overcoming an obstacle that had long prevented them from making progress. Reaching for whatever lay at hand in the prevailing chaos, and combining fragments with no intention of creating something beautiful, but simply tossing together scraps from a need to express themselves, in a gesture recalling Antaeus renewing his strength by touching the earth, they produced delightfully refreshing works which cleanse the viewer's eye and mind jaded by too many metaphysical demonstrations.

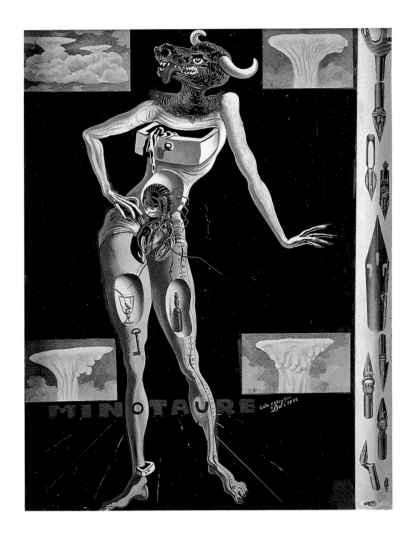

THE aim of the Surrealist enterprise was to denounce commonplaces, shatter clichés, and, in defiance of every norm, classical canon of taste, and critical standard, to replace conventional reality with a "surreality" that could engender new relations between beings and the space in which their actions occur. The 1934 collage entitled *Bathers* by the Czech artist and poet Jindrich Styrsky, who that same year joined the Surrealist movement with his companion Toyen (also a collage artist), is a good illustration of this program. The artist turns an insipid chromo into an image which is as distressing to the eye as to the mind. Thanks to the ease with which one thing can be substituted for another in a collage, an idyllic scene is transformed into a nightmare. The innocent games of two young women (an erotic stereotype derived from Mannerist painting) release monstrous fantasies. Under a canopy of timeless leaves by the edge of a forgotten, sheltered pond, beneath the flawless youthfulness of two female bodies, viscera are engaged in their slow work. In a cruel baring of the process of repression by which the mind protects itself from death (according to Freud's theories), Styrsky's collage reminds you of a surgical operation. The uncomfortable realism of what amounts to an evisceration is amplified by the contrast between the cruelly descriptive treatment of the grafted organs and the mincing banality of the illustration taken from an album of popular pictures. Unlike what happens in Max Ernst's collage novels, with their atmosphere of pervasive uncertainty, the element of perturbation is easily identified here. The metamorphosis of the two figures' innocently playful movements is both irreversible and brutal. Their skin is turned sadistically inside out and their relationship is made to appear, in the light of new psychological theories, bestial and morbid. Despite its affected seductiveness, the idyllic chromo is unable to resist the irruption of extreme violence.

Jindrich Styrsky
(1899-1942)
Bathers, 1934.
Collage.

"BORN November 27, nineteen hundred and three /I have no God, no master, no monarch/and no civil rights." The Belgian artist, E.L.T. Mesens, who wrote these lines, embodies the libertarian, playful spirit that the recent revision of ethical values by the Dadaists had inspired all over Europe during the 1920s.

Though he started out as a composer and was an ardent admirer of Erik Satie, who taught him irreverence, Mesens gave up composing in 1923 after discovering, together with his friend René Magritte, the magic of Giorgio de Chirico's painting. He took up poetry next because he felt it had more scope. Then, in 1926, wanting to give a visual presence to the inventions of his brain stimulated by the new current of metaphorical freedom, he started making collages. His early works skilfully combine Magritte's disabused sense of humour with the influence of Max Ernst and Man Ray. Then Mesens, obliged to make a living, became an art dealer in London and organized exhibitions. For thirty years he championed the Surrealist cause: he collected Surrealist works, exhibited Surrealist painters, and was a vital link between the London group whose leader he was, his Surrealist friends in Brussels, and the Paris Surrealists. He took up collage again when he retired in 1954. Inspired by the work of Kurt Schwitters whom he visited in England, where the German artist lived in exile, Mesens paid increasing attention to chromatic values obtained by arrangements of fragments as well as to the formal suggestions contained in materials subjected to various kinds of wear and tear. These late collages of Mesens, which remind us of music scores, echo the passions of the artist's youth. Typographic characters, words, repetitive forms, squares and circles, replace isolated notes and suggest a music muffled by the privacy of a daydream. The 1958 *Landscape* shown here expresses the artist's characteristically languorous elegance. The subtle arrangement of the vertical strips of paper with their modulated patterns

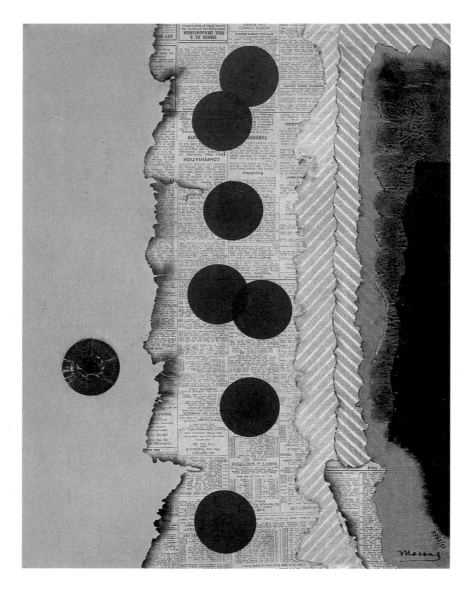

E.L.T. Mesens
(1903-1971)
Landscape I, 1958.
Collage.

104

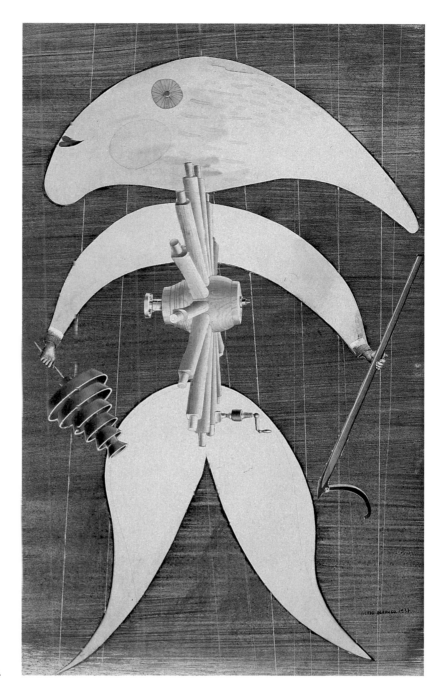

Victor Brauner
(1903-1966)
Personage, 1937.
Collage and gouache.

creates a rhythm that blossoms slowly on the page, a rhythm rendered more languid than ever by the delicate rips and traces of the flame that seared the papers' edges. Against the background of this listless pavane the sombre shrilling of a solo instrument reverberates, a run of notes echoed on the left by the final sustained pause of an absurdly mortal star releasing its last light.

VICTOR Brauner did very few collages. His remarkable visionary powers blossomed in the sinuous lines of a pictorial idiom that seemed to spring from his dreams and in overlapping forms whose incandescent colours exhibit an inner energy that is sustained alternately by a desire for erotic union and the Angst of a primordial separation. Like Hans Bellmer and Yves Tanguy, the Surrealists with whom he shares the deepest affinity, Brauner manipulated collaged elements, taken from manufacturers' catalogues, popular illustrations, and common advertisements, to create a distance and al-

leviate the tension that usually fills his images and to give them a more relaxed appearance, a gayer, strangely ironic buoyancy.

In the bizarre *Personage* which Brauner assembled in 1937, the artist seems to be simultaneously exorcizing the latent drama in the figure and amusing himself with a playful construction. By exhibiting the unconscious mechanism governing the figure (the large wheel hub placed in the vital centre of its body) and by supplying its aggressive drives with weapons that are clearly alien to its nature, as if they had been placed in its hands by another will, Brauner takes the edge off any anxiety that the brutal dissection of the atrophied, disproportionately elongated limbs might otherwise have produced. Briefly setting aside the totemic masks and magical powers whose bodily drama (with its mythical impregnations, births, and metempsychoses) is the subject of his painting, he uses collage to display a harmless puppet. By showing us the wires that hold it up, he reassures us: this is only a game, the stakes are make-believe.

André Breton, Yves Tanguy
and **Jeannette Tanguy**
Exquisite Corpse, 1938.
Collage.

Modern Art in New York, still bears the traces of an enthusiastic conversation between the artist and the publisher over lunch. As soon as he got back to his studio after the meal, Picasso picked up a print of the Minotaur (one of the many such prints and drawings in his work) and cut it out roughly. In a gesture of emblematic independence, he then combined it with a paper doily and some tin foil which were souvenirs of his luncheon with Skira. Thus, as was so often the case with Picasso, a private occasion was immediately transmuted into a mythical image.

Picasso had already used the pasted paper technique back in 1928 in one of his earliest depictions of that mythological beast imprisoned in the dark labyrinth of passion, the Minotaur, who was one of the masks the artist used to disguise the questionable side of his nature as a man and a painter. The crude cross formed by the rectangles of cheap monochrome paper helps to contain the rapid charcoal lines which seem inhabited by an incredibly violent energy. But at the same time the presence of simple, unprepared materials (excepting the barely discernible moiré of the blue) reflects the background of anxiety and inner turmoil underly-

In 1933 Albert Skira began publishing *Minotaure*, a luxurious art review devoted to revealing both the breadth and variety of the Surrealists' activities, as well as their scornful rejection of all systems of classification, all barriers, whether racial, linguistic, or moral. During the seven years of the magazine's existence an impressive array of bizarre objects, exotic discoveries, revolutionary technical innovations, and daring theories were presented in its articles and reproductions, like curiosities in a Mannerist collection. Painters, poets, photographers, scientists, historians, and philosophers jointly mapped out an imaginary geography between the review's covers. Guided by the logic of dreams and desire, analysis and reportage, they explored the intricate vastness of man's inner continent. The thread that they followed through this labyrinth was the fine line between the instinctive animal forces in man and the timeless, ubiquitous resources of the mind which manages to contain, though unfortunately not always, the excesses of blood. Skira commissioned a different artist to do each cover of his review (there were thirteen issues in all). The first cover was given to Picasso, who threw together one of his sublime improvisations. The assemblage that served as the maquette, now in the Museum of

Pablo Picasso
(1881-1973)
Cover for *Minotaure*, Paris, No. 1, 1 June 1933.
Collage.

ing the drama of this monster who is cruelly deformed, as though warped by desire and the curse of a sin it can never expiate.

Pablo Picasso
(1881-1973)
Minotaur, January 1928.
Charcoal and pasted paper on canvas.

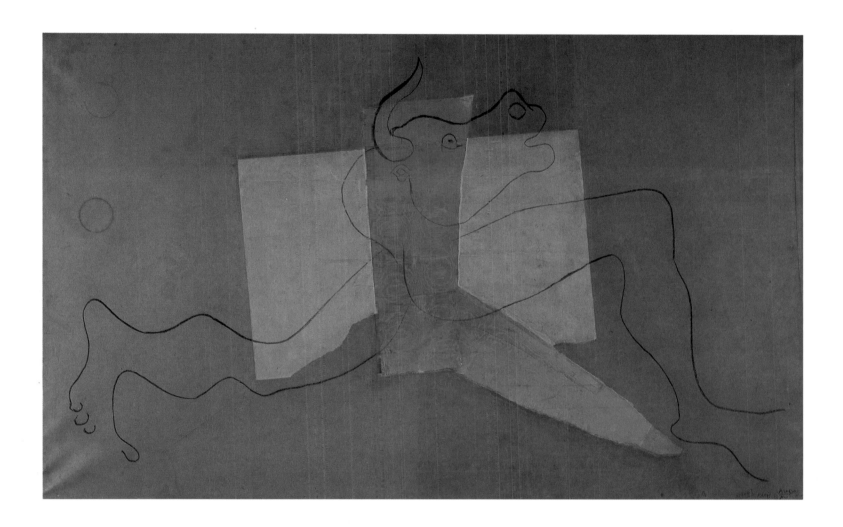

JOAN Miró spent the summer of 1929 in Catalonia. at Montroig, the village of his chi dhood, where he made a small series of almost arrogantly thrifty pasted papers. It is as if the hitherto generous springs of his oneiric inspiration had dried up and he had suddenly been visited by doubts about the colourful ease and bravura of his painting over the previous five years. There are no feminine arabesques in these collages, no pliant forms, no dazzling colours, no women, no birds, no stars winking in the depth of boundless space—in short, none of the lyrical effusiveness of his earlier work. These negatives signal a crisis of confidence: the artist no longer trusted the splendid spontaneity of his own touch. There is something brutal about the way Miró's art, one of the most euphoric oeuvres of the 1920s, one of the freest, airiest of Surrealist fantasies, was suddenly defeated by "the most rugged reality you can embrace," the peasant's sense of palpability that sooner or later triumphs over artists who, like Rimbaud, choose to become "v - sionaries." Both an instinctive artist and one filled with doubts, Miró was to experience more than one such slump during his career. But none was as radical as the 1929 crisis which, in what was perhaps a rever-

sion to the Dada spirit of some of his earlier paintings, made him long for "the assassination of painting" (llustration page 98).

There is not a glimmer of humour or cheerfulness in these austere inchoate constructions of 1929. These sparest of images seem scorched by the summer sun, the leaden noon heat that seals the earth and incinerates everything in sight. The most humble of materials, the most abrasive textures (emery paper, rough cardboard, aluminium foil, tarred canvas), are crudely assembled, randomly combined, in harsh concretions that look as if they had been manhandled. Either the artist deep in his pit is paying scant attention to the materials he is slapping together with seeming blindness, torn, soiled substances that are weighed down with his passion to express himself. Or the work itself is meant to be the labour of a merciless summer devastated by the sun's glare. Is this Gérard de Nerval's "black sun of melancholia"? More likely, it expresses the Spanish *nada*, that concrete nothingness, that absolute bedrock which every imperative comes up against from time to time, that simulacrum of birth/death which enables the artist to collect himself and pursue his flight.

WHAT artist's oeuvre seems as natural as Arp's? His sculptures, for example, which are better known than his graphic work, have an ease, a formal amplitude, that seems to bridge the gap between art and life. Yet they do not attempt to imitate life's externals; instead they translate the inner growth of the biological process, the secret germination and respiration which underlie the gradual transformation of living beings. Similarly, the pasted papers which Arp began producing as early as 1932 reduce the distance between the creative act and the toil of nature. "The torn paper is as beautiful and perfect as nature. Birth and death are natural and untragic to it," Arp wrote. Few artists in a troubled time have combined such certainty with such

an extreme artistic modesty; few oeuvres have displayed such a tranquil resistance to a rising tide of anguish and death.

Arp begins by tearing up a sheet of paper, a rejected drawing or print, a prepared gouache surface. He then scatters the fragments randomly on a pre-glued support. Gently adjusting them with his fingers or making invisible alterations with a brush, pencil, or file so as to bring out the fragments' flaky texture, suggest attractions, or restore a missing organic equilibrium, he discreetly and almost blindly brings his forms to blossom on the page. At the end of the process, he wipes off the excess glue, allowing the smudges and streaks thus produced to take on an accidental and seemingly inconclusive quality within the work. As Arp emphasized on several occasions, the impulse comes from within the work itself; it stems from the essence within the forms, the active core in the colours. The artist lets himself be guided by the image emerging beneath his fingers. He places his trust in the mysterious movement which ripples through him, a movement he does not control and that flows onto the page like breath from the lungs or water from a spring. There is no reflection on the artist's part, no planning; there is no artistic pride in making a work of art. What these admirable little improvisations which seem about to crystallize into constellations (or else to disintegrate into particles—one will never know which, and it hardly matters) express is the inner workings of life itself. Just as nothing occurs in nature as we intend it, Arp says that art is not there to impose a message. It is enough for it to translate, anonymously and modestly, the secret palpitations in the heart of the biosphere.

Hans Arp
(1887-1966)
Torn Drawing Duet using elements by
Sophie Taeuber-Arp, 1947.
Torn and pasted paper on cardboard.

YET it would be wrong to assume that Arp's work excludes all premeditation. He was too much of a creator to be willing to surrender every advantage of the artistic enterprise to chance. One has only to look at the *Torn Drawing Duet*, which Arp made in 1947 using one of his wife Sophie Taeuber-Arp's works, to understand that his sensitive vigilance extends to chance itself: the violence with which the fragments have been torn and the freedom with which they have been scattered on the support are counteracted by the inner necessity created by the artist's intervention. His redistribution of the fragments even bolsters the work's linear firmness, while the tenuousness suggested by the tears (further increased by the indefiniteness of the diluted colours) provides an ideal ground for the ballet of attractions and repulsions. Loyal to the rules he had set for himself in 1915, Arp puts chance

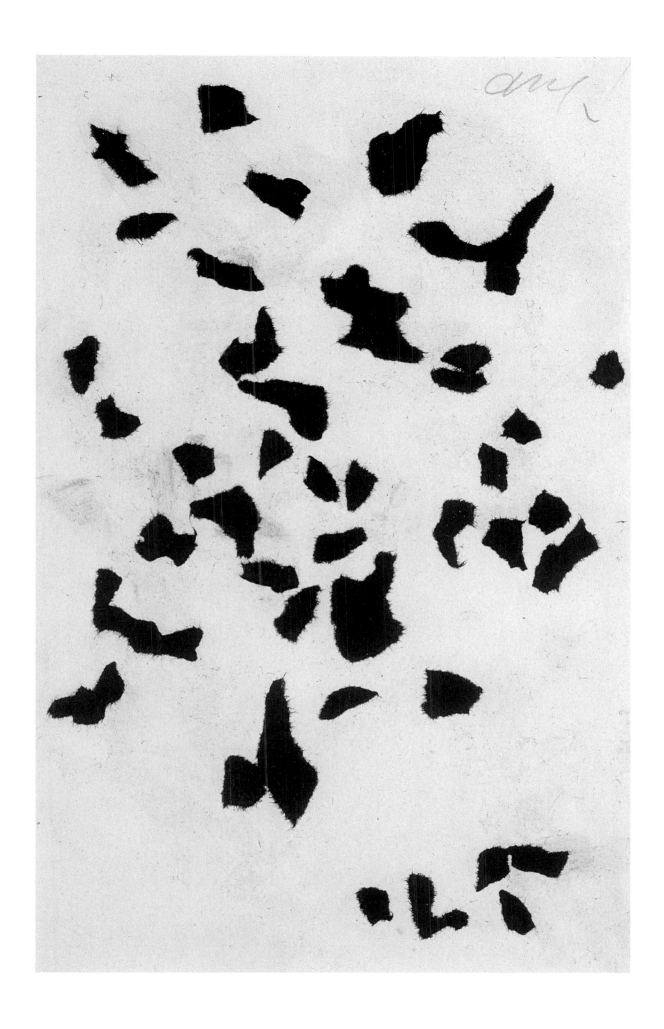

on his side. Such a receptivity to the aleatory suggests that there are laws above and beyond the artist which use his emotions to articulate a mysterious higher reality. That is why the artist's touch is only minimal in this collage of torn papers, seems in fact wholly absent. To want to add to nature—to re-produce—is absurd, Arp felt. He believed, on the contrary, that the artist's task is simply to produce works the way nature grows fruit, flowers, clouds: by taking part unobtrusively in the invisible work of the universe, by giving birth to truths that are at once gratuitous and inevitable.

Henri Matisse
(1869-1954)
Two Dancers, 1938.
Study for *Red and Black*.
Paper cutouts and thumbtacks.

SCULPTING LIGHT

DURING the first three decades of the twentieth century, the radical and indeed irreversible changes which affected the way art pictured the world were mostly the result of joint undertakings, often adventurous and far-reaching in scope. Both in science and the fine arts brilliant experiments and daring theories were generated and sustained by group discussions, by the exchange and cross-fertilization of ideas across frontiers and fields of activity, alliances, controversies —and even schisms.

Almost all of the artists mentioned so far in this book were members at one time or another of a movement which involved them, whether they liked it or not, in the ongoing polemics of history. But there is one outstanding exception to this general rule: Henri Matisse. Here was an artist who, by sheer temperament and strength of mind, proved to be a law unto himself. From the beginning, he purposefully resisted any contamination of his art by the kind of biographical factor or doctrinal consideration which most of his contemporaries, even the most independent and single-minded, were caught up in.

To Matisse, the artist's *raison d'être*, his essence and sole justification, lay in his work, in daily confronting its specific demands and coming to grips with the hidden or neglected powers of his own means of expression. He gave himself totally to his art, doggedly working his way through doubts, going from fresh start to fresh start, never rejecting tradition, seldom succumbing to the specious allurements of spontaneity.

On the contrary, the remarkable sense of freedom in his work, of *spacious freedom*, rests on careful observation, purposeful intellectual growth, and endless sketches and exercises which subordinated the painter's deft touch to the sense of mystery he was forever trying to express. He felt and thought his way steadily forward. The ideas which guided him were matured and fleshed out gradually; they came into existence only in the process of painting. His art was not shaped by external considerations or preoccupations. It imposed itself slowly, unconsciously, as the only path open to the artist.

From this standpoint alone, the gouache-painted cutouts of Matisse's final years are quite different from the pasted paper works and collages of artists who preceded him. He never used scissors to declare war on painting; his paper assemblages never deferred meekly to the laws of chance. Any approach by way of the aggressive or the random was foreign to his temperament. His cutouts, with their fine, full-toned colours, are immediately distinguished by the easy confidence with which their outlines declare volumes and shapes, giving them a formal amplitude which you do not find in anything done by the Cubists, Dadaists, or Surrealists. Similarly, the way Matisse employs the cut-out technique to simplify forms does not correspond at all to a regression of pictorial language, but (like traditional techniques such as drawing, painting, and sculpture) it seeks to express as accurately as possible what the artist really feels in his daily confrontation with the model and indeed with all the, to him, ever fresh and stimulating beauties of the visible world.

Matisse first began to use cutouts systematically in 1943, but he had already experimented with them. He had taken them up to design theatre costumes in 1920; to create an architectural fresco in 1931-1932 for the Barnes Foundation at Merion, Pennsylvania; for magazine cover illustrations; and to design maquettes in 1937-1938 for a ballet, *Rouge et Noir*, choreographed by Leonid Massine on a score by Shostakovich.

In the course of each of these ventures, his pragmatic mind had immediately grasped the advantages of this technique: the saving in time and space, the rationalized work method. It allowed him to shift forms and seek out relationships without changing the ground on which he worked, to play with chromatic intensities and balance timbres so as to obtain a satisfying harmony, one that reflected his long-standing concern with subordinating objects of external reality solely to the picture's internal imperatives. Moreover, the cut-out technique gave him the freedom and time to bring his figures to life by adjusting the space, the airy blank surface, surrounding them. It enabled him to compose every part of his pictures according to proportions and colour contrasts which effectively expressed, not objective facts, but his own feelings about the model.

The revelation of possibilities offered by the cut-out technique, which the painter had not been fully aware of in his earlier pasted paper experiments, struck Matisse precisely at the moment when he began to use this procedure systematically. He realized that it could settle a question that had been bothering him for years: how to arrive at a cohesion which, in nature, weds contour to surface, the legibility of line to the physical intensity of colour. By cutting out shapes from large gouache-painted sheets of paper prepared by an assistant, he was able to combine two hitherto distinct actions in a single, simplified gesture. With a pair of scissors you could "draw in colour," as he put it; you could "resolve the eternal conflict between line and colour" which had been at the heart of his work since the beginning. The difficulty of fitting a coloured field into a previously outlined form was at last surmounted, and the artist's hand, thanks to the scissors it held, could inscribe arabesques directly on a coloured material. "Scissors," he said, "can acquire more feeling for line than pencil or charcoal." And again: "Each particular group of colours in a cutout has a particular atmosphere. It is what I call the *expressive atmosphere.*"

Furthermore, the unification of line and colour in a single gesture guaranteed accuracy, freshness, and truth—a truth to feeling that enthralled Matisse. Themes, forms, and space now acquired a buoyancy in his work, a luminousness, a power to wrest themselves from the oppressive grip of darkness. These qualities seem all the more remarkable when you compare them to the despair and sombre cruelty in the works of his contemporaries. Matisse often spoke of the joy, the sheer exhilaration, that he got from cutting out forms with scissors, the feeling of freedom and confidence that comes with carving shapes in a coloured mass, as if the hand, impelled forwards by the emptiness it is cutting into, simply has to yield to its own impulses, has to glide over the curves set by the artist's feeling for the model.

To Matisse, who associated scissoring with airy wheelings and swoopings of birds (an arabesque-like writing that cancels out shadows and time in an endless coming and going of feathered wings), the cutout had all the untrammelled freedom, precision, and flexible, natural equilibrium of flight. It was both an arrow piercing emptiness, sustained (so to speak) by a void, and a space vibrating from the arrow's flight. In July 1937 Matisse had already experienced a similar excitement in an airplane between London and Paris. The flight above clouds had seemed wonderfully relaxing to him, had given him a sense of freedom and weightlessness; but more than anything he had felt surrounded in the upper air by a dazzling transcendent light which expanded his sense of space beyond any-

thing he had ever imagined. Trying to recapture this experience of respite from urban drabness and the poison of human politics, Matisse, on returning from another kind of journey—"rising from the dead as if by miracle" after the nearly fatal surgery he underwent at Lyons in the winter of 1941—devoted the last thirteen years of his life to producing a steadily increasing number of gouache cutouts. In the end, these paper works were to replace his painting and sculpture altogether.

The first stage of his conquest of a new pictorial space was *Jazz*, one of the most beautiful illustrated books of this century, published by Tériade in 1947. It contains twenty plates reproduced by means of stencils made from cut-out maquettes. On the pages facing the brightly coloured illustrations, Matisse wrote out, in his own handwriting, some thoughts and comments about his own art, which he composed especially for this edition. Oddly enough, he considered the book a failure, despite the success it encountered. One reason was that, at the time the book was published, he was involved in new experiments with cutouts. These *papiers découpés* were better than the old ones, he felt, because they preserved his scissor strokes in all their original freshness. Even though the stencils in *Jazz* appear to have accurately rendered the chromatic relationships in the maquettes, the reproductions undoubtedly lost some of the sensitivity and vitality of the originals. True, the public had received the book favourably, delighting in that "penny plaything" the artist had kept himself busy with during bouts of insomnia brought on by physical pain and anxiety, but Matisse himself had already moved beyond its imperfections, with a series of further cutouts which enabled him to elaborate on and interiorize the results of his discovery.

The improvisations in *Jazz*, the book's syncopated character, its bursts of energy fuelled by alcohol (a practice which the artist was reluctant to repeat too often), were soon absorbed in cut-out experiments which seem less attractive but are in fact attempts to further refine forms, to condense visual objects into signs that express their essence. The circus and music hall themes give way to a less frenzied, more serene expression of joy—a meditated, deeply buried, but soon overflowing joy triggered by images of the South Seas that came to life again, after lying dormant for fifteen years in the artist's memory. The intense hues of the Pacific haunted his imagination to such a degree that the last few plates in *Jazz* (the *Knife Thrower*, the *Swimmer in the Aquarium*, and the two *Lagoons*) are invaded by a fluid vegetation substituting its natural luxuriance for the ephemeral, nervous,

Henri Matisse
(1869-1954)
Seated Blue Nude III, 1952.
Gouache on cut and pasted paper.

well-rehearsed equilibrium of tumblers and acrobats. Responding to this gift, this miraculous dispensation of youth in old age, Matisse experimented with cutouts in an attempt to create a so far unparalleled sense of freedom and ease which, like memory itself, could shine through time-bound forms, intensify their colours, and (thanks to the synthesis allowed by the cutout technique) blend the undeniable simplicity of the outer world with the flowering within the work of art. Before long Matisse had almost forgotten about oil paints and canvas and was doing only cutouts—birds, plants, sea animals, every sort of creature that floats untrammelled, drifting in its specific element, pliant, buoyant, free, with stately, arabesque-like movements, without encountering the slightest resistance: jelly fish, sea weeds, "splendiferous" fish cradled by tides, mermaids riding waves, clouds and sails skimming before the wind, monkeys and girls peering out from a yielding tangle of leafage. Dancing, which Matisse had always loved as the most direct expression of *joie de vivre* (for in dancing the human body is wrested gracefully from the tug of gravity), was made to express the very breath of life in his last gouache cutouts. Here the artist's dancers seem to have forgotten the physical effort that underlies what passes for weightless motion.

Nonetheless, the reason why the cutout (whether used independently or subordinated to another technique, like stained glass, ceramics, or tapestry) became Matisse's favourite procedure towards the end of his life is not just that it permitted him to pare down the creative gesture to its bare essentials or that, again like memory, it can clarify and simplify the vocabulary and syntax of picture-making. Obviously the cutout allowed him to get back in touch with a concept of space which he had already worked with years before, at the beginning of the century, notably in the large painted panels of *La Danse* and *La Musique*, where arrestingly contrasted juxtapositions of flat surfaces saturated with bright colours and treated frontally in defiance of all the conventions of academic painting and realism, resulted in cancelling the illusion of depth and replacing it with a musical reading of an image consisting wholly of abstract rhythms embodied in schematic, contoured figures.

Matisse's lively interest in the decorative arts (with their absolute frontality and their assertion of two-dimensionality) was strengthened by his experiments with gouache cutouts, where ornamental motifs could be endlessly repeated, switched, and varied until the artist was satisfied that he had reached the right equilibrium. The kind of large-scale decoration that evolved in Eastern civilizations, especially in Islamic

art (to which Matisse had very early shown a great sensitivity), obliges the viewer to approach the work of art on two different levels—conceptual and melodic. By condensing the profusion and movement of visual reality to a few simplified universal signs that anyone can recognize at first glance, then by arranging these signs into algebraic rhythms (permutations, repetitions, reversals or mirror-images), the language of decoration opens up the spectator's perceptions to an intangible reality whose limits are confused with the invisible, if not the divine.

It is the Oriental example of serene contemplation that Matisse strove to reach in his last gouache cutouts. He

Henri Matisse
(1869-1954)
Sails, 1946-1947.
Gouache on cut and pasted paper.

Henri Matisse
(1869-1954)
The Parakeet and the Mermaid, 1952.
Gouache on cut and pasted paper.

transcended the besetting preoccupation with contingencies, distinctions, and hierarchies that has so often encumbered Western art. In vast compositions he assembled on the walls of his improvised studio at the Hotel Regina in Nice (the *Swimming Pool*, the *Parakeet and Mermaid*, the *Negress* the *Large Decoration with Masks*), isolated elements such as palm trees, fruit, stars, and swimmers proliferate, spilling over and filling whole walls (well before contemporary "environments"). By allowing a powerful radiance to shine through the space between each brightly coloured form, these splendid private frescoes cancel the blank opacity of plaster and brick walls and suggest a limitless space opening up beyond them, an "immense, completely white landscape bathed in brilliant but undazzling light." Here was something of the same "increased spiritual space" the artist had experienced in his exhilarating flight from London to Paris back in 1937.

These paper thin enclosures ornamented with leafy forms, which Matisse secluded himself in towards the end of his life, were like the Persian hangings that fluttered in front of his windows, curtaining him from the endless dazzle of sea and sky. They made his Riviera studio a garden of dreams, and the Mediterranean light that filtered through was the radiance of paradise.

Twice, though, Matisse broke through this screen. The first time was when he decorated the Dominican Chapel of the Rosary at Vence (1947-1950), and decorated it with fervour. Here he created a feeling of sacred boundlessness by combining pure colours in a stream of intangible light that shone through stained glass windows, with simplified lines inscribing their beautiful shorthand on immaculate white tiles. This

synthesis, a result of the artist's mastery of the cut-out technique, blends in a single movement the purity of a linear style that excludes anecdote and shading with an intense luminousness that bathes and spiritually transfigures the chapel space by dissolving its confining architecture.

If there is one figure that deserves to be placed at the centre of this luminous space in Matisse's last works it is the female nude. The artist had always viewed the female anatomy with deep feeling, akin to awe and reverence. From his earliest work on, he had depicted it resting, entranced with the mystery of its own beauty, in unforgettable expressions of eternal youth and the joy of living.

Thus the four *Blue Nudes* of 1952 are linked to the countless seated, recumbent, and sleeping nudes, fauns, and dancers that inhabit the paradisiac landscapes of the painter's earlier pictures. But nothing surrounds them now. There is no decorative setting to explain their presence; they are animated solely by a tension between simplified arabesques and saturated colour zones barely rippled by the flow of regular brushstrokes. Their outlines, shaped by scissors in an ultimate effort to fuse abstract forms and concrete appearances, vibrate against a rising tide of blue; a restful, ethereal, infinite blue such as you see on the domes of Islamic mosques; a blue that seems to relieve volumes of their last ounces of weight and convert them into free-floating sources of intangible radiance. They seem to alight on the retina—these four blessed, memorable nudes—as if they were being projected there by a purely spiritual light.

And so the eye, taking in their commanding presence, comes to forget the slow patient labour, the hesitant repeated touches, which characterized the painter's

work from the outset. Instead, the viewer is arrested and overwhelmed by a feeling that he is beholding forms that are as decisive and tangible and straightforward as statues—with the difference that they are carved directly in colour. Every salience, every depression, every break increases the inner radiance of the figure. The sense of space communicated by these cut-out pictures seems greater than anything in reality, for it possesses to the full, as Matisse himself observed back in 1949, the "vastness of [the artist's] imagination."

In spite of Matisse's misgivings about *Jazz* (1947), and in spite of an uncharacteristic feeling of disquiet that some of the plates produce on the viewer, few illustrated books have ever achieved such a perfect cohesion of theme (a "crystallization of memories of the circus, folktales, and my travels," as the artist put it) and technique. The frontal space, analogous to the picture plane in a painting, where Matisse's performers enact a magical frieze is determined by the artist's choice of medium, gouache cutout. Over an underlying architecture of large coloured rectangles, which remind you of sliding panels or flats in a music hall or cabaret, a series of pirouetting figures, whirling under bright lights in a glitter of paillettes, describe tense, weightless arabesques.

You feel immediately that no other technique than scissors sculpting crisp forms in the very weft of colour could have evoked so vividly the conjurer's world where sudden changes of lighting, multicoloured costumes, and rapid shifts of emphasis create an enthralling yet ephemeral show, a celebration of childish delight, barely ruffled by a few genuine thrills of terror. But already that one-syllable word *Jazz*, so close to *joy*, evokes (with the twin zebra stripes of its final pair of consonants) the rhythmed excitement of dancing, the syncopated hip thrusts of swing music, the tapping feet and clapping hands of big band musicians. *Jazz* with its twenty plates may be described as an album of shows; it is divided into magical chapters whose intensity (just barely attenuated by the "background music" of the handwritten pages between the illustrations) grows with the increasing difficulty of the performances it depicts. It reaches a brief, carefully prepared climax—in a return to total silence—as the artist performs an acrobatic solo on a tightrope as thin as the cutting edge of a knife blade.

And, in fact, the *Knife Thrower*, depicting the crucial moment when, in his nightly gamble with death, he is about to hurl a knife and the audience holds its collective breath, is profoundly symbolic. Surely the confrontation between the circus artist and his partner, who faces him, motionless, fascinated by the violence in his eyes, is a metaphor for the artist, scissors in hand, striving to silhouette the ideal contour of his model? Then too, can you forget that, only a few years before, Matisse had had a brush with death, when operated on for an intestinal occlusion, and had been saved only by the skill of his surgeon?

The perilous balance achieved (at the cost, indeed, of almost superhuman efforts) in the illustrations for *Jazz* actually seems to release, in a curious sort of whiplash reaction, an upsurge of repressed memories which had been locked in the artist's unconscious for close to fifteen years. In the midst of the clamour and forced gaiety of the circus, images of the South Sea islands Matisse had visited in the early thirties suddenly blossomed, and they are more intense than the limelight of the ring. They are free, weightless images. The years have softened the contrasts between colours, the hard edges of lines.

Thus, at the very time when the artist's scissors are still feverishly trying to capture the tense motions of a juggler, the gravity-defying leaps of a horsewoman, new forms are beginning to appear in his work. They are unobtrusive at first, but as we turn the pages of the book they begin to spread. In the last two plates, *Lagoon I* and *Lagoon II*, they take over entirely—fluid, feminine forms floating up from the depths of the artist's memory. A long forgotten joy seems to expand their outlines and slow their bright flowering. In the *Knife Thrower* the lazy swaying of palm fronds patterned on the surface of the work has the effect of placing the drama of the encounter between the circus artist and his passive partner in a space enlarged out of all proportion, a space where the victim, isolated by her serene beauty, is forever out of reach.

Henri Matisse
(1869-1954)
The Knife Thrower, 1943-1946.
Maquette for *Jazz*.
Gouache on cut and pasted paper.

The Knife Thrower, 1947.
Stencilling.

Henri Matisse
(1869-1954)
The Acanthi, 1953.
Gouache on cut and pasted paper.

118

PART TWO

COLLAGE AND ITS DOMINION

Except for one glorious interlude, from 1943 to 1954 when Matisse was working on the gouache cutouts which came as the crowning achievement of his career, the golden age of the pasted paper seems to have ended with the last collages of Max Ernst, Joan Miró, and Hans Arp.

Not that there was any lack of novel, ingenious, or insolent inventions in this field; on the contrary, the collage technique was used widely by contemporary artists of every stripe on both sides of the Atlantic. It would be tedious to list all those who used it in one way or another, either for casual experiment at irregular intervals or in a sustained manner. Still, the aura of passionate discovery and the intuitive confidence of the first pasted papers was gone. The challenge to traditional painting and obsolete ways of thinking and seeing, a challenge repeated daily for more than ten years now, was weakening; and the formal imperatives that distinguish any new artistic procedure seeking to establish itself were losing their strength. Little by little, the pasted paper was becoming a standard item of avant-garde language, unexciting and passively accepted. Its original violence, its sudden intrusion into art, its almost physically irritating assault on the eye: these were softened, blunted by the innumerable glosses and imitations it inspired.

As a result, during the decade of the fifties, when the lessons of Cubist and Dadaist collage were being reinterpreted and attuned to the sensibilities of a new generation, the pasted paper came to serve as an auxiliary technique, an additional means used in conjunction with other procedures, rather than as a revolutionary weapon, an instrument of liberation (which it had been without interruption from 1912 to 1925). Its allusive rhetoric, based on discrete signs and subtle metonymic shifts from part to whole, from alert consciousness to elusive dreams, began to lose ground to the mid century artists' need to transcribe, without paraphrasing or resorting to any kind of aesthetic "filter," the unvarnished reality of their place and time.

In the aftermath of World War Two, the full horror of the Nazi genocide, the stunned realization following the bombing of Hiroshima, the apocalyptic visions of smouldering ruins and rows of dead bodies all bore witness to the absurd and monstrous truth of what human and technological progress can lead to. And the onus of this knowledge required painters who were sensitive to the reality of modern man's destructive madness to come up with infinitely more violent pictorial means than those which had been used up until then. A dramatic iconoclastic brutality and rebelliousness triggered by this reality were grafted onto what we tend to forget today was a deep, in some cases ineradicable trauma. At the same time, increasing urban growth brought increasing poverty in squalid inner city and suburban landscapes through which the artist roamed, torn and helpless, in search of subjects and materials that could express the solitude of the city dweller. Motorways, sprawling industrial projects and new housing developments, helped to alter man's relationship with his environment and the way he looked at the world. The frantic pursuit of affluence, glorified by powerful advertising soliciting the eye at every moment and from every wall, made it a vital necessity for those who lived in cities (and soon even in deserts) to own a car, a refrigerator, a vacuum-cleaner. The popularity of the movies, with their stereotyped heroes and vulnerable princesses; the acquisitiveness spawned by the satisfaction of short-lived, forever intensified and rejuvenated pleasures: the outcome of all this was a new repertoire of images and, in art, a need to respond to it with a new perception of space and time—one that was more fragmentary, convulsive, and insatiable than ever before.

Confronted with an accelerating expenditure of energy, scissors seemed too fine-fingered an instrument, ill suited to express modern men's anxiety and need to communicate. Likewise, though the artistic vision of the new generation was still steeped in the principles of collage as defined earlier in the century, and though the daring innovations of Cubism (not to mention Schwitters' redemptive poetry and the Duchampian concept of the found object recycled as an art work) were still operative concepts, mere paper and paste now seemed inadequate for the task at hand. What the artist glued to canvas was no longer just the world's litter, but now included new objects as well, plastic and chrome artefacts of a civilization engrossed in instant gratification.

The art work was now a glossy, only just barely ironic reflection of modern society's affluence, when it was not the arena of a ruthless struggle between the artist and a polymorphous material (mineral, vegetal, animal, liquid, gaseous, volatile) savagely assaulted and questioned in what amounted to a physical skirmish fought with shears, axes, saws, vices, pickaxes, blowtorches, metal punches—and even a rifle fired by Niki de Saint-Phalle at goatskins filled with paint.

Never before had there been such an outpouring of torn images, ripped canvases, cut-out, eviscerated, crushed, compacted objects. Paint was squeezed onto canvas straight from the tube, or dripped from a punctured can; it was liberally poured onto the support; it agglutinated in dribbled slippery nodes which the artist would work with a palette knife or directly with his fingers; and in this impasto all sorts of extraneous items were embedded: shredded fabric, old cardboard, wood scraps, wire netting, shards of glass, all manner of wreckage and waste spangling the surface of these pictures. And unlike Cubist pasted papers which seem to push up against the picture plane, as if they were struggling to break into the third dimension; unlike Surrealist collage which appears to tunnel down in search of unexplored subterranean reaches; these assemblages seem, on the contrary, to cling to the debris of a world cast adrift. A world that can no longer be grasped except by probing its dissociations, its unexplained juxtapositions, its contradictions. When objects and fragments are not simply deposited in a box or scattered on the floor (linked by connections so tenuous that their very unrelatedness trivializes them and, at the same time, affirms the fact that they are being redeemed by an artistic gesture), they are cemented, nailed, bolted, riveted together; put in bags, wrapped, tied, sealed, soldered. But whether they are scattered or bound together, they seem to claim a forgotten dignity; attractive or unattractive, rich or poor, magical or humdrum, permanent or perishable, they remind the eye of their manifest *thingness*.

The avant-garde of the fifties, which rejected the lyrical evasions of *art informel* and showed but little sensitivity for the arcane subtleties that delighted the last initiates of waning Surrealism, was loud in calling for a popular, easily understandable, totally contemporary art capable of expressing the almost exclusively urban landscape, the environment these artists knew and experienced daily.

Accordingly, they invented a simple, forthright pictorial idiom, one that was deliberately foreign to the norms of good painting and good taste, one that allowed them to state clearly the problems of a society swept in a dizzying vortex of unrestrained productiveness and technological record-setting; a society whose dynamics, giving rise to ever new and greater and more insistent needs, was imperilling the basic equilibrium of life itself.

Thus the art of assembling objects, which, stemming from collage, came into its own in the fifties, expressed, even as it in turn was proclaiming the demise of the dominant aesthetic of the previous generation,

Christo
(1935)
Surrounded Islands,
project for Biscayne Bay,
Greater Miami, Florida, 1932.
Collage in two parts:
fabric, pastel, charcoal,
pencil, enamel paint,
crayon and photostat.

a salutary intellectual vitality, a creative imagination strong enough to withstand the entropy that was jeopardizing both the production of images and the way art was being looked at (far too passively); strong enough, in fact, to create art works from a civilization in crisis.

The abundance and variety of art works steeped, from 1950 on, in an accumulative sensibility shaped by the tradition of Cubist and Futurist pasted papers, by attitudes and behaviour inherited from Dadaism (with its fundamental recognition of the value of actual materials), by Duchampian creative fortuitousness and the negation of artistic personality: in retrospect this multiplicity revealed the full scope of the plastic procedure discovered in 1912 by Picasso and Braque. As a matter of fact, it was in these same mid century years that several general studies of collage appeared, and several exhibitions devoted to the art of the pasted paper were organized, placing this influential invention in a broad historical perspective.

The combine paintings of Robert Rauschenberg are often cited as prime examples of the art of assemblage. And it is true that the seemingly haphazard presence

of miscellaneous textures and procedures (painting, drawing, photography, newspaper clippings, typographical characters and numbers, found objects and materials) defining the freefloating, uncharted space in Rauschenberg's works is a striking expression of the new poetics of the absurd. Rauschenberg evokes the glamour and the indigence of the urban environment, with all its sounds, colours, and movement; there is a subtle criticism implicit in the artist's casually indifferent gesture scattering, without any premeditation or censure, the signs of decadence registered by his all but dispassionate mind. But by now the artists and works that were being influenced in one way or another by the new rhetoric were legion: Joseph Cornell's puzzle boxes; Louise Nevelson's secular reliquaries; Jasper Johns', Jim Dine's, and Tom Wesselmann's object pictures; Andy Warhol's trivialized serial images; Richard Stankiewicz's playful solderings; Richard Hamilton's and Edward Kienholz's installations; Arman's accumulations and "destructions"; Spoerri's trick pictures; Tinguely's explosive machines; John Chamberlain's and César's compressions; Christo's wrappings; Martial Raysse's constructions using plastic, neon tubes, pieces of mirror, etc.; Erró's panoramic views; Jiri Kolar's crumplages and rollages; Enrico Baj's mechanistico-military masquerades; Jean Dubuffet's fragile and diminutive idols made of oakum, sponge, driftwood, his portraits fashioned from butterfly wings; Antonio Tàpies' sandy pictures, with their still visible prints and tracks; Alberto Burri's burlap pictures; Hains', Villeglé's, Dufrêne's, and Rotella's "poster art"; Allan Kaprow's and Wolf Vostell's performances, and so forth.

And yet, in spite of everything, though the *spirit* of the pasted paper did in fact shift during the fifties towards something else—assemblage—and though it lost its specific character, the art of scissors and paper and paste did not disappear altogether. A few painters, whose work was less flashy and more introverted than that of most of their contemporaries; a few artists naturally drawn to the poetry of small, intimate occasions, kept it alive; adhering strictly to its rules, they invented new solutions which renewed its appeal.

ONE SUCH painter was Nicolas de Staël. He brilliantly exploited the possibilities offered by scraps of paper and cardboard of differing texture and thickness, saturated with pure colours (particularly the blues and reds which were always "in his head," as the artist wrote to René Char in 1954). His compositions, with their large flat areas of colour, are charged with a suppressed violence—and in some cases this violence is released in sudden bolts which cleave the work in two; some of these pictures were made for their own sake, others were conceived as maquettes for tapestries or book illustrations (reproduced by lithography or wood-blocks).

In this unpublished project a scattering of tiny coloured particles, made vibrant by the irregular tearing of their thick cardboard, expresses the airy shimmer of light's dazzling radiance. Space seems to burst forth between these specks of coloured matter, as if (to cite Jacques Dupin's apt comment apropos of the artist's drawings) it is "able to act only by breaking and enter-

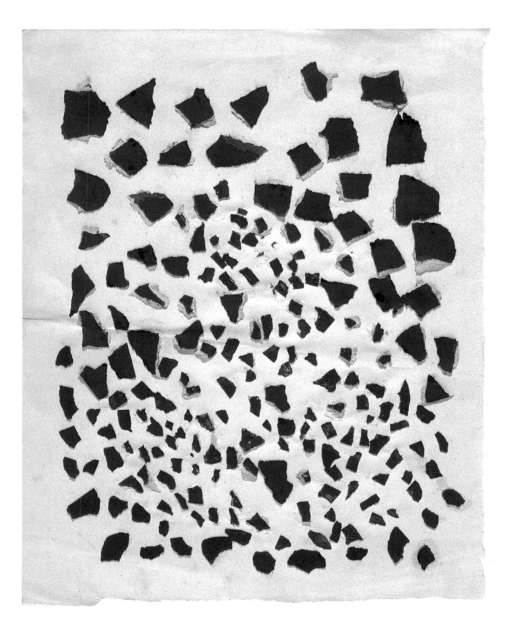

Nicolas de Staël
(1914-1955)
Blue and Red Collage
on White Ground, 1952-1954.
Primed and torn cardboard.

122

Marcelle Cahn
(1895-1981)
White Disk, 1953.
Pasted paper.

Friedrich Vordemberge-Gildewart
(1899-1962)
Collage, 1946.
Pasted paper.

THE LITTLE pieces of torn paper used by Friedrich Vordemberge-Gildewart (who, with Marcelle Cahn, was a member of the Circle and Square movement from 1930 on, and kept to geometrical abstraction all his life) are not glued to the support any more solidly than hers. In fact, they are less solidly glued—it almost seems that you would blow them away if you breathed on them.

After World War Two, came a change. He stopped making austere constructions of rhythmical vertical and horizontal lines and began a series of "dropped" papers: following Hans Arp's example, he used a random process to compose his visual scores. But unlike Arp, Vordemberge-Gildewart seems to have given thought beforehand to the patterns on the materials he selected, so that the formal relations between fragments, even when they are very remote, counteract the anarchy of arbitrary scattering. The artist's detached manner, his subtle sense of humour, his sensitivity to shifting light, turn these unassertive pasted papers into works charged with something oddly mysterious. The artist himself seems to have been quite aware of this, for he once remarked that "collage is more valuable than any combination of daring and imagination."

ing, is able to respond only to gaps and crumbling lines, to the unhindered circulation of the void between fragments, in the interstices between disjoined forms and divided elements."

THE TECHNIQUE of the cut-out pasted paper provides Marcelle Cahn's deeply meditated art with a sort of melodic counterpoint whose imponderable magic is increased, if anything, by its restraint. The artist's scissors add nothing to the circles and rectangles which enhance her best paintings and drawings; but the physical presence of scraps of paper slightly unstuck from the support, the luminous inflections produced on the surface of the work by almost involuntary accidents arising from the action of the glue, and the drawn lines which structure the added fragments, prevent the work from sinking into monotony. It is enough for the artist to shift the grid of her ruled paper by a few degrees, to redirect the linear structures or reverse their orientation, to slightly modify the thickness of her materials, for the space surrounding these fragile two-dimensional mobiles to begin to revolve.

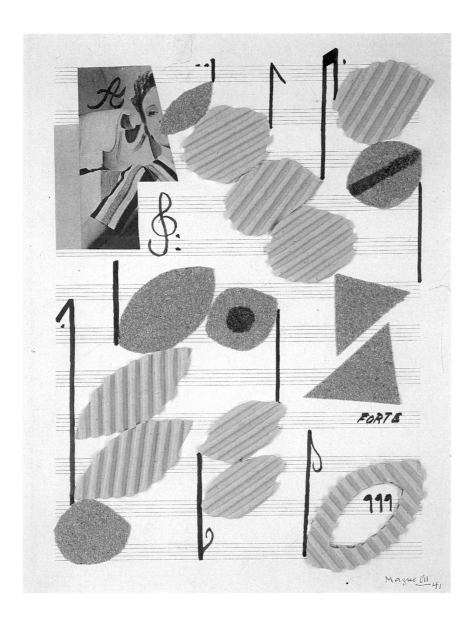

Alberto Magnelli
(1888-1971)
Collage on Music Paper, 1941.
Emery paper, corrugated cardboard, illustration,
pen and ink.

WITH Gaston Chaissac, a provincial artist, the intricate art of the pasted paper recaptures the childish, folksy flavour it had in the beginning, before modern artists made it one of the instruments of their radical pictorial vision. With him, there is no visible intention of producing an aesthetic break; his pasted paper compositions (like his paintings on cardboard, wood, linoleum, stone, and plaster) are candid expressions of his poverty and marginal status. Like most other *naïf* and *brut* artists, he created art out of whatever came to hand, unconcerned about the dos and don'ts of academic painting and passing fashions. And in all likelihood, what the artists—foremost among them, Jean Dubuffet—who, accepting this self-taught village dauber in their ranks, encouraged him and gave him friendly advice, expressed, above and beyond a legitimate admiration for his work, was their own yearning for an authenticity which they themselves no longer possessed, an I-don't-give-a-damn attitude as unqualified as it was unaffected.

True, Chaissac's collages are less daring and irreverent than some of the pasted papers of earlier artists. But that is precisely what makes them so delightful: for Chaissac includes decorative wallpapers in his collages simply for the pleasure of it; he fits bits of paper together, like puzzle pieces, not to create a shock ef-

fect but merely as a way of recalling childhood games; and he does all this with the visual assurance of a consummate artist familiar with the tensions between forms and the joy of colours. With, in addition, a sovereign freedom that allows him to switch with impunity from laughter to terror, from an impish grin to the innermost stirrings of the soul.

ESTÈVE practised the art of the pasted paper at his country home in summer, in the Berry region of central France where he was born and grew up. In fact it was in the very room of the house where he was born that he set up his country studio in the mid 1950s. And it was there, in the stimulating familiarity of his native air, that he now took to collage, as if to counterbalance the studied architecture of his oil paintings and the tensions of his watercolours; and he brought to it a spontaneous imaginative verve rooted in the natural profusion of rural life as well as in the treasury of his private mythology.

The fantastic creatures of his collages are inseparable from the procedures that engendered them: what sustains the inventiveness of this artist (who looks on with wonder and delight as unexpected, yet oddly familiar blossomings spread on the sheet of paper be-

124

fore him) is his choice of papers, either untreated or coloured with paint spread with a brush or ink applied in energetic pen strokes; the forms he cuts with alternately dreamy and lucid, controlled scissors; the way he assembles fragments according to the affinities and contrasts between them and to the promptings of texture, form, and colour.

And so the artist's hand and eye, tending their garden, bring forth hybrid strains instinct with vegeta patience and birdlike alacrity. Masculine and feminine forms intertwine in these new life forms, amorously at times, more usually drolly; exotic refinements combine with rustic frankness; the precision of sunlight mingles with the occult cycles of the moon. Yet, Estève's most accomplished pasted papers (the *Feather Tree* of 1965 unquestionably belongs in this category) further accentuate this innate ambiguity by rendering the equilibrium between the fragments more precarious than ever. Like glass particles in a kaleidoscope, the piquant figures devised by Estève's whimsical imagination are shaken, almost disabled, by the convulsion which sweeps them.

Gaston Chaissac
(1910-1964)
Sullen Look, 1959-1960.
Painted, torn and pasted paper,
gouache and oil.

The fact is, we expect them to collapse at any moment; yet this fear is immediately laid to rest by the promise of new figures, further metamorphoses. Thus the instability of these painted burlesques stems less from a real threat than from reality's unlimited capacity to renew itself, to transform its own disequilibriums into affirmations of vitality.

THE PIECES of paper (those vehicles of colour) which Le Corbusier pasted to sheets of drawing paper have an essential function for this artist who chose building as his vocation: they structure space. Firmly glued, either as found or covered beforehand with a coat of pure bright gouache, these newspaper clippings, these fragments of discarded drawings and wrapping paper establish the organic structure of the image over which the artist's hand then traces sensitive arabesques with a pen. The symbolic presence of these luminous blocks, solidly moored to the margins of the page or else distributed over the picture surface with a lively feeling for formal rhythms and chromatic reverberations, enables Le Corbusier to shift from one plane to another, to capture the motility of the external

Jean Dubuffet
(1901-1985)
Pearly Garden, June 1955.
Assemblage of butterfly wings.

◁ Trembling Ground, 1959.
Assemblage of imprints.

world and bring it into the picture. Just as lines, in prehistoric cave paintings, may stray from the colours they are meant to delimit, or wander from the strict truth of profiles and contours yet express a truth of their own, so too, in Le Corbusier's collages, there is an interaction (at times parallel with the picture plane, at other times seemingly perpendicular to it) between snug, exact, often dramatic lines and coloured masses which convey a generous and restful impression. From the tectonic tension animating the image, restraining extemporaneous impulses without altogether suppressing them, there arise certain of the fundamental architectural principles which Le Corbusier strove to concretize: the idea of contrasting solid and transparent walls, the notion of free circulation within a constructed space, unobstructed passage from up to down, front to back—as free as the way the eye slides from one point on the horizon to another.

THE SERIES of collages on music paper which Magnelli composed in the country near Grasse, in southern France, where he secluded himself early in World War Two, is a relaxed interlude in the long line of experiments he conducted in this medium between 1936 and 1965. The gentle humorousness that colours these pictures probably owes something to the fact that Hans and Sophie Arp were Magnelli's neighbours at the time. And yet, in spite of their anecdotal side and the facility with which they were composed, these pasted papers are as carefully thought out as the abstract pictures the Italian artist made with rough-and-ready materials, such as packing paper, string, envelopes, corrugated and reinforced cardboard, bookbinding leather and paper which evoke both the world of books and the correspondence the painter carried on with his friends in a time of silence and separation.

Le Corbusier
(1887-1965)
Bull, 1962.
Pasted paper, gouache, pen and ink.

▷ **Maurice Estève**
(1904)
Feather Tree, 85 C, 1965.
Pasted paper, coloured inks, and blue crayon
on yellow ground.

In addition, Magnelli's pasted papers give one an exact measure of what the painter meant by composition: with the control and self-discipline of a true craftsman, the artist elaborated music scores, using elementary optical givens—strict forms, sober colours, miscellaneous textures—which release their music only when combined in contrasting or harmonious relations; only then do they attain a degree of tension sufficient to communicate their harmonious vibrations to the sheet of paper as a whole. And that is not all: Magnelli brings to his formal orchestrations a remarkable sensitivity for those forthright, ungraceful sounds evoked by coarse burlap, ordinary wrapping paper, and abrasive sandpaper. With these materials he suggests directions, velocities, pauses on the picture plane.

And so his compositions have a restrained, sober, sturdy music of their own. By the simple fact that they are the outcome of a procedure strictly followed, they invite us to "listen" to them with the internalized, private concentration we experience when reading or listening to a poem.

A MAN of free, unwarped judgment, Jean Dubuffet was attracted by all forms of expression that lie outside the schools, outside the conventions of history. The methods that appealed to him were those in which the magic touch, the play of fancy and untrained spontaneity, counts for more than skill or knowledge or taste.

So it was that about 1953, together with his friend Pierre Bettencourt, he rediscovered those butterfly-wing compositions which had occupied the leisure of anonymous art lovers in the late eighteenth century. But the very scarcity of the main ingredient soon led him to replace the variegated patterns of delicate insects by small pieces of inkstained and spotted paper which he combined with a drawing previously made. On the sheet then appeared those tiny, spirited manipulations which were carried through the very tissue of the image itself. These he soon developed into a series of complex lithographic works and assemblage pictures consisting of cut-out pieces of canvas.

IN THIS collage of 1959 entitled *Trembling Ground*, Dubuffet did not content himself with merely reproducing a landscape. That was not his way. His unswerving concern was to bring us, willy-nilly, into intimate contact with the invisible order where those metaphorical transmutations occur which weave the pattern of appearances.

Painting, for this artist, one of the major originals of the twentieth century, is not an arrangement of forms and colours for the pleasure of idle minds. It is an in-

128

strument of spiritual knowledge and communication. And he considered that, for such purposes, it has distinct advantages over speech and reason, inasmuch as its power of conviction rests on the immediately tangible and tactile arguments of actual matter—paints, paper, or whatever. This matter, as if dissolved in the pale transparency of the wash, is like a deposit brought down from above to the ground, irrigating it and gradually flowing off into its deeper strata. But in order to give the impression of a quiet subsidence of matter, a downward slide at once followed by a compensatory and equally natural upgrowth towards the surface, like the secret fulfilment of an organic cycle, Dubuffet draws on the simplest means at his disposal:

imprints, that primal expression of the artist's hand, combined with the new procedures of assemblage. This sedimentation taking place before our eyes acts upon the small detached blocks of paper, bringing them down in an inexorable fall as graceful nevertheless as the slow scattering of sand in water suddenly stirred.

And one comes to see that this drift of elements, their uncertain form changing as accidents occur, their apparent instability, refer to that unseen inner growth, that germination of energies, that confused and precarious stirring of life deep within beings and things, which Dubuffet's inventive sensibility was ever intent on revealing.

Robert Motherwell
(1915)
Mallarmé's Swan, 1944-1947.
Pasted paper, gouache, and crayon
on cardboard.

A COUNTERPOISE TO LYRICISM

It WOULD seem at first glance that the assumptions underlying action painting, a movement of non-geometric abstraction which emerged in the United States towards the end of World War Two, must necessarily exclude the syntax of the pasted paper. The dry, detached technique and the principle of manual anonymity inherent in *papiers collés* seem squarely opposed to the action painter's passionate physical involvement with painting, the practice of automatic gestures analogous to the Surrealist system of automatic writing (in the work of Miró and Masson, for example), the fluidity of paint poured on canvas, the use of a thick impasto shaped by the artist's desires and rages. Insofar as it pretends to be an "immediate undoctored transcription" of the artist's personal emotion at the moment he is confronting the blank canvas, action painting cannot burden itself with the delays, however slight, which scissors and glue inevitably occasion.

Hence this paradox: although for decades the new procedure invented by Braque had been conducive to the most daring optical experiments, it seemed inadequate to convey the expressive urgency of American artists in the forties and fifties. Enthralled with their own subjectivity, intent on an immediate outpouring, these artists thought that unconscious flights could be faithfully rendered by movements of the hand and arm; they believed that speed, energy, and working on a large scale guaranteed both plastic accuracy and emotional truth.

But then new ways of painting were discovered, forgotten techniques were resurrected, simpler and more malleable materials were invented. These made it easier to improvise and, more significantly, they brought back the painter's touch, which the pasted paper had, if not altogether eliminated, at least dissociated from the artist's perceptions. The psychological outpouring that resulted from the hand moving freely to its own aggressive or redirected impulses (the fondling touches, angry stabs, sudden leaps and convulsions of the brush) took the place of the anonymous chance materials of collage in its heyday.

Does this mean that, given these unfavourable circumstances, the pasted paper ceased to be used altogether? Hardly. For though it had by now lost the experimental character it once had in the eyes of its discoverers, this immensely rich rhetorical system (or at least isolated aspects of it) survived here and there in the works of the artists of the forties and fifties. Among the young artists then eager to found a new pictorial tradition on irrepressible subjective impulses and on their perception of a boundless lyrical space whose centre was both nowhere and everywhere, many had been marked by Cubism, either directly through Picasso or indirectly through artists Picasso influenced (like Léger or, more radically, Mondrian). Despite the violence with which these painters externalized their innermost urges, despite the occasional excesses resulting from the confrontation between painter and canvas (an indispensable theme of this school), they never stopped being concerned with order. They had a sure instinct for structure and plastic rhythm, and this kept them from expending their energy on some kind of decorative vitalist art.

And it is precisely at the point where the two opposed forces of control and lyricism come together that the pasted paper and cutout can play a meaningful part by summoning the eye back to the picture plane and so putting a break on what would otherwise be a space expanding out of control.

The difficulty is: how are you to reconcile the apparently intellectual requirements of structure with the outpouring of instinct and impulse rushing to take physical possession of the canvas?

This was the problem that faced a number of American artists when they discovered the liberating possibilities of automatic procedures imported to New York by exiled Surrealists. So it was that the young Robert Motherwell began to experiment with the pasted paper in 1943 after seeing the international collage show at Peggy Guggenheim's Art of This Century gallery.

Motherwell's work is a good example of the conflict we have been speaking of. His dynamic touch and surging colours are still firmly contained inside a grid of cut-out paper fragments which organizes the pictorial surface. The resulting spatial arrangement clearly owes much to the rigorous constructions of Picasso's experiments with the same technique around 1915.

Robert Motherwell
(1915)
Elegy for Salvador Allende, 1975.
Poster collage on gouache-painted paper.

▷ **Willem de Kooning**
(1904)
Collage, 1950.
Oil, lacquer, and thumbtacks on cut papers.

The pasted paper technique (which complements painting and even contributes its own solutions to it) satisfied a need in Motherwell for equilibrium between spontaneity, elegance, and a yearning to escape the here and now. At times this gave rise to an art that was almost classical: for example, *Mallarmé's Swan* (1944-1947), a composition which consists of delicately coloured vertical strips just barely ruffled by a breath of pure lyricism.

WITH time, as he grew older, Motherwell's pasted paper works evolved towards greater formal freedom and bigger dimensions. Taking large sheets of paper coloured with flat tints, and using flattened cardboard cartons, torn envelopes and scraps of posters that stand out like ragged flames against a painted monochrome background, Motherwell expanded pictorial space boldly and freely, opening it up, in airy compositions, to the winds of inspiration. Making no attempt to disguise tears in the materials he used, or the original purpose of those materials, he created a dramaturgy based, in some cases, on his own memories and private allusions, in other cases on universal myths and political events of burning relevance.

The large pasted paper entitled *Elegy for Salvador Allende* (1975), a moving lament for a brutally extinguished hope for a juster, more humane society, centres around a torn lilac-coloured poster announcing a political rally—a symbol of free speech being trampled by the military junta which overthrew Allende, a flash of bright colour exploding like a starburst in the cold grey fog descending on the Chilean people and its legitimate aspirations.

IN HIS paintings, Willem de Kooning sometimes collaged cutouts scissored from his own working sketches, and though this was not frequent, it nevertheless illustrates a basic aspect of his work.

The pasted paper, with him, is a tangible expression of the irreducible incompleteness which the artist's creative urge tried to eliminate with dogged persistence in canvas after canvas. In his pictures reality eludes your grasp, shies away. It is an intimation, not an entity. There does not even seem to be an image to hold on to; and though the current of the artist's feeling may be strong and true to its source, inevitably, as it spills over the sheet, it encounters resistance, it comes up against obstacles which stem its flow and turn it away from its natural slope.

Now the essence of collage is to reveal visual breaks, to lay bare the inescapable obstructions which prevent the artist from grasping the totality of his work in a single movement, and to disclose the places where line becomes colour, the junctions and intersections

that rhythm the uneasy relations between fragments. What is more, a collage by its very nature can be dismantled at any stage of its creation and reassembled at will without ever causing a definite solution to emerge—a solution, that is, which is better than any other solution.

In this 1950 collage (a splendid assault on painting by painting) thumbtacks, clearly visible on the surface of the work, suggest that the present state of the constantly shifting chaos which the artist is forever trying to organize can only be provisional. Other transformations await; new overlays and permutations are always possible. The tacks are the only fixed points in the picture; the eye fastens on them and collects itself before plunging back into chaos.

Reworking the image to equate it more closely with the primal convulsion which brought it forth, wielding his brush like a sword, splashing rich, sensual colours on the canvas; withdrawing, repositioning, and re-engaging his forces in an ongoing creative process, de

Kooning reminds you of the painter Frenhofer in Balzac's famous story *Le Chef-d'œuvre inconnu*. But unlike that fictional artist who, in a desperate quest for perfection, blindly destroys the masterpiece which he thinks he is on the point of completing, de Kooning is lucid and surprisingly systematic in his surrender to the forces driving him. He believes—or he hopes—that, by bravely confronting the endless transformations of the figures he paints, he will eventually catch a glimpse of whatever it is that moves him to paint, the ever elusive mystery behind the passionate turmoil on the surface of his pictures.

Lee Krasner
(1908-1984)
Lame Shadow, 1955.
Collage of paper and oil on canvas.

Franz Kline
(1910-1962)
Untitled, II, c. 1952.
Brush and ink and tempera on cut and pasted paper

LIKEWISE, in Franz Kline's work collage seems to redistribute the cards in what is already, in part, an open game. When a player places a card face up, he obliges the next player to rethink his strategy and improvise a new combination. So too with the fragments overlaid on this composition consisting of a few simple brushstrokes: they intrude roughly on our perception of the work and break up its optical continuity. A few fluid sweeps of black ink on a page ripped out of a telephone directory, and the sudden wilful hiatuses of the pasted fragments with their torn edges, produce a semblance of order and suggest an additional possibility (one that is about to be superseded by a further possibility) of a new pictorial space. The swarming printed lines further accentuate the impression that the collage is a wobbling ongoing process. The proportions of the underlying linear architecture are blown up by the bold brushstrokes, and the result is that the eye loses its familiar bearings and finds itself absorbed in an optical vortex where earth and sky, horizon and foreground, are jumbled in a whirlwind of movement approaching a catastrophic climax.

Wolf Vostell
(1932)
Fiestas de la Merced, 1962.
Dé-collage.

UNGLUING AND TEARING
OR THE ART OF THE HOARDING

IF EVER there was an art that did not need to take to the street, it was the singular movement launched in France and Italy in the early fifties by the so-called "poster ungluers."

Art of this kind did not need to be made; it was already there, in the city streets, waiting to be discovered. It was on walls, on construction hoardings, in subway stations, on billboards in railway stations and suburbs. Artists like Raymond Hains, Jacques de La Villeglé, and François Dufrêne (in Paris), and Mimmo Rotella (in Rome) appropriated a treasure trove of images in a hundred urban locations. Alien to the theoretical nitpicking of tachism, *art informel*, and other abstractions, they proceeded to found a new "naturalism." But nature in the countrified or parkland sense had nothing to do with it. Theirs was an urban naturalism, leading them to discover the hitherto unnoticed beauty displayed on billboards—fragile, shortlived frescoes exposing their garish colours, giant lettering, and shock images to the vagaries of weather and the vandalism of passersby. And so this new breed of wandering artist repaired to the street, equipped with capacious bags and spatulas, and, on foot or in vans, they tracked down surprising visual effects which were the result of chance, malicious acts, and gratuitous depredations.

To these plastic accidents they sometimes added their own contributions (a rip, a pasted addition). At other times they simply collected the most interesting torn advertisements they could find and later, back in their studios, they divided the spoils. Some fragments were mounted on canvas as is, and were then dated and indexed; others were subjected to further mistreatment, systematic or accidental; and still others were reinterpreted, turned back to front, reorganized in original compositions.

The mere act of roaming through the city, tramping the streets and alleys, and appropriating fragments of crude reality (other artists about the same time were picking through garbage cans and visiting city dumps) made the "ungluers" accomplices of the nameless vagrants, outcasts, rebels, and harmless conspirators who seek furtive, inarticulate vengeance for all the slights they have received (or fancied they've received) from a shameless, selfish, uncaring society.

Thus even before the "ungluers" exploited the graphic possibilities (the gaps, scratches, revealing openings) offered by the torn poster's brief splash of colour, they proclaimed their solidarity with the anarchist and hoodlum. Their works have all the heedless and playful insolence of rioting students, all the pithiness of that language of the gutter which is apt to be common to the urban worker and children of the streets.

What is more, the art of ungluing posters (a considered art, calculated and pondered over, quite the opposite of Art Brut) is a wellnigh perfect synthesis of the various traditions handed down by the pioneers of the pasted paper.

t is an art, therefore, which embraces the Cubists and their partiality for real objects and substances, their punning use of printed syllables which create allusive verbal textures within the image; the Futurists and their urban concerns; Arp's free play of chance forms and rhythms; Schwitters' passion for textures and substances; the invention of an intellectual viewpoint that transforms a found object into a work of art; a crisp critical approach that takes art out of its usual context, as it does with the early Readymades of Marcel Duchamp.

The art of ungluing posters is an anonymous art that anyone can understand and master. Still, there are noticeable differences between the artists who practised it. As its colours, forms, textures, and substance are drawn from the medium it uses (and that medium consists of found materials), it requires no manual skill. Everything depends on the artist's eye: its role is crucial (although not all critics understood at first just how crucial), for it selects the materials that make up the work.

IN HIS "anonymously lacerated" works lifted as is from Paris walls, Jacques de La Villeglé emphasizes the lettering that is scrambled, broken up, engulfed in a vortex of swirling, torn, overlapping fragments. In this flurry of contradictory, confusing bits of information, a printed letter is a bolt of lightning, an explosion of colour, a particle of an allusion to an event that took place in a time that will no longer ever make sense.

François Dufrêne
(1930-1982)
Half-Sister of the Unknown, 1961.
Tattered remnants of posters mounted on canvas.

The *Fiestas de la Merced* by the German artist Wolf Vostell articulates a more pessimistic view of the publicity environment: printed announcements, subjected to a mutilating compression of names, dates, and events, disintegrate and, in the decaying substance of the poster, yawning holes open.

WITH Raymond Hains the tearing of the material seems more direct and dramatic. It expresses anger, clawing and ripping the object of the artist's fury, leaving its violent signature on savaged posters. The works he showed at the *France déchirée* exhibition at Galerie J in Paris in 1961 are explicit about the rea-

sons which prompted him and his circle to commit acts of blasphemy and sacrilege. And yet the dark feelings that sought an outlet in visual violence have something in common with that surrender to instinctual urges, that temporary blindness, which possessed the Abstract Expressionists when they tried to grasp the inner truths haunting them. A sense of equilibrium, of effective visual breaks, an innate knowledge of the potential that lies in colours, appears to guide the hand of the artist—that mute, irascible, nocturnal iconoclast who, independently of any school or aesthetic trend, succeeded in producing the sort of fusion of act and feeling which the Abstract Expressionists struggled to achieve.

▽ **Mimmo Rotella**
(1918)
Queen Christina, 1962.
Torn posters mounted on canvas.

FRANÇOIS Dufrêne, himself an errant child of the Paris streets, is fascinated by what lies beneath posters, by their "hidden decors," to use the words of this inveterate and consummate punster. In his eyes (and ears) every truth has a sort of twin (*Légende, les Andes*) or, to borrow from the title of the work shown here, every unknown woman has at least a half-sister. In the excavated layers of what happens to lie between poster and wall there is a palimpsest (or rather the shreds and tatters of a palimpsest) whose original message has been irretrievably lost.

Soon growing tired of the thankless archaeologists' task of trying to decipher a crumbled or garbled message, the viewer's eye is drawn to lovely accidents, and torn fragments, and swarming random forms which seem to quiver still with the violence implicit in frayed paper; it takes in the delicate tints, the gorgeous shot silk of mildew, the rings, stains, foxings, bruises, and blushes that blossom in the uniform hues of the linings of walls.

Raymond Hains
(1926)
Peace in Algeria, 1956.
Torn posters mounted on canvas.

IN HIS first, abstract period, the Italian artist Mimmo Rotella explored the plastic resources of the art of tearing posters: the layerings, gouges, scratches, and lacerations; the ambiguous overlappings; the cardboard stiffness of paper soaked in starchy paste; the blisters and wrinkles caused by rain and glue; the distortions of lettering; the still pools and flying arrows of colour; the dynamic rhythms of stripes and slashes; the languid stains; the bleeding tints; the alternating bright and faded tones. But after 1960 recognizable figures appear in his spiderwebs of torn paper: glimpses of faces, winking eyes, smiles, signalling hands, parts of naked human anatomies, flash bulletins and allusions to current events, billboard idols making guest appearances on a phantom stage. To the attractions of an art based on action he added the magic of a fresh view of things; a laying bare of whole segments of forbidden, obscure, cruel or comical truths. But the heroes and heroines of this genial reporter of the quotidian are the demigods and demigoddesses of Cinecittà (that factory and bastion of dreams symbolically located on the outskirts of the Eternal City). Thanks to the stripping away and the surprising juxtaposing in the art of poster tearing, these screen deities seem paradoxically protected from the desire of ordinary mortals, yet at the same time they are joined in improbable and extravagant marriage.

139

Jasper Johns
(1930)
Flag above White with Collage, 1955.
Encaustic and collage on canvas.

BRINGING ART AND LIFE TOGETHER

THE OVERWHELMING presence on the American art scene, beginning in the mid forties, was the New York School, better known first as Abstract Expressionism, then as action painting. It brought with it and imposed the religion of the vital impulse, attaching prime importance to the physical act of painting. This art of non-geometric abstraction, powered by ever upsurging undercurrents, flourished with scarcely a rival for about a decade, until the tide began to turn.

Peaking around 1950 with Jackson Pollock's violent and highly original cosmologies, Abstract Expressionism had led by then to a sharp reaction by younger American artists. The latter opposed the wild trances of action painting with a new way of looking at things, dispassionate, free, mobile. They absorbed all forms of urban reality, whether derelict or hyperbolic or accelerated. Adepts of a new "objectivism," they were especially sensitive to the influence of Marcel Duchamp, whose intelligence, irony, and enigmatic silence helped them to escape the rigidities of what was in part a return to a more academic concept of art. The French artist's example taught them that art is a matter of inventing a critical attitude towards an ever changing world (a world, moreover, in which they themselves were forever changing), not of producing "tasteful" objects or images that pretend to be visual equivalents of the artist's inner violence.

Viewed in this light, the work itself becomes an objective event, no more and no less threatening than any object or event in reality. It presents itself as a conflict of fleeting, violent impressions; a large coherent segment of the world, or an arbitrary fragment or magnified detail, or an equivocal image which confuses reality with an advertisement.

The breadth and vitality immediately shown by American Pop Art and its deliberately simplified idiom, often blown up to the hyperbolic dimensions of advertising and movie language, hardly seems compatible with the pasted paper. For the latter is mainly a procedure for an artist working in the privacy of his own room or studio, a painter more concerned with the internal relationships of a composition and the way images function than with transcribing a reality that reflects technological gigantism. The art of assemblage was a useful but auxiliary tool for American painters active in the early fifties.

Yet this did not prevent some of the rising generation of artists from yielding to the plastic attractions of paper fragments, from combining the specific advantages of this procedure with other techniques and mediums. It would be unfair not to mention the original contribution of artists like Robert Rauschenberg and Jasper Johns, simply because their work does not correspond to any convenient definition; or to overlook the delightful narrative works of Romare Bearden (to give but one example out of many), simply because they do not fit into any of the established categories of art history.

ANYWAY, few works of art match the classifications that professors use; they have a way of escaping as soon as you try to fit them into a pigeonhole. Consider, for example, the *American Flags* by Jasper Johns, a series that has given rise to contradictory interpretations. The flags are not really Pop Art at all (except for the actual theme), for the impersonal manner the artist uses to neutralize the subject's all-too-evident symbolic meaning, and so reduce it to a strictly pictorial fact, conducts the viewer beyond the somewhat simplistic views most people have about this movement. The apparent banality of Johns' choice of the American flag for his subject (which some link with flag-waving nationalism and others interpret as a gesture of irreverence towards his country) serves as a pretext for subtle variations on simple forms and colours; variations that, on a more sophisticated level, question the relationship between reality, images of reality (that is, the pictures themselves), and the confusion of identities inherent in the symbolic process.

Instead of overlaying torn fragments of newsprint, photographs, or advertisements on a composition painted beforehand (as earlier painters tended to do), Johns uses collage to question the image from below, as if the pasted papers were belatedly surfacing or striving upwards towards an impossible completion. A vague submarine turmoil produces turbulence on the surface, a shimmering of just perceptible nuances; signs of wear and tear on the surface (fissures, lacerations, stains that break up a flat picture and tone down its geometry) serve to transmute a trivial image into a visual celebration.

But at the same time, crimes and accidents arranged in wavy columns that show through the waxy layer of hastily applied pigments proclaim a decay and obsolescence that threaten to undermine the proud stability of what the national flag stands for. The empty space beneath the flag might be a kind of negative flag, an anti stars-and-stripes. A dreary, silent waste covering the facts of reality—fossil facts embalmed in encaustic—it would seem to represent, in the eyes of the artist, that deathlike rigidity which must sooner or later turn the great American myth into a thing of the past, unless America manages to rid itself of its illusions about the power of progress, its dangerous, limitless self-confidence.

TOM WESSELMANN'S approach to the pasted paper, which is explicitly and avowedly in the tradition of the Matissean cutout, is altogether different. The hard edges of Wesselmann's figures and his limited colour range (flat, acid, at times garish tints which saturate the picture surface) propose a new visual mode based on simplified, exaggerated images that are projected indiscriminately on the retina.

These collages, as it happens, were made under particularly difficult conditions, made in a studio which was so cramped that the artist had to assemble them on his knees. And so it is perhaps natural that they speak of the cluttered space that presses down on the inhabitants of large cities in America and of the visual inflation that assails your eyes there.

The heavily accentuated lines of Wesselmann's figures, the emphatic contouring of this or that part of the anatomy (breasts, belly, lips), the crude realism of the pose, the frigid sensuality of the model who comes straight out of a fashion magazine—all this creates a sense of discomfort, of an impersonal overabundance, that inevitably influences our reading of the work. Beneath the apparent facility of Wesselmann's images one discerns a critique (one that is not only unsparing but grows increasingly ironical in the *Great American Nudes* series) of the ubiquitous photographic model (a snapshot or close-up, often crudely framed, taken from a distorting angle and overexposed to produce washed-out colours) which pretends, with spurious objectivity, to record an intimate moment—whereas in fact all it does is reduce life to a set of stereotypes (objects, cliché sentiments), to a pointless, superficial clinging to the passing instant.

BUT THE artist who evinced the greatest determination to bring art and life together was Robert Rauschenberg, beginning in the early fifties.

What interested and attracted him was the current imagery of popular culture in America, and his use of raw materials in his first audacious constructions can perhaps be traced back to his early training at Black Mountain College, in the hills of Asheville, North Carolina, under Josef Albers.

His visual material is drawn from the chaos of the street, the poverty and overcrowding of the tenement, the windblown waste of the vacant lot; his pictures are vibrant reflections of the confusion and anxiety that fills you when your perceptions are cast adrift in the vortex of the actual. Each of Rauschenberg's combine paintings is an attempt to create an event. It is a totally free, open work where chance constellations of materials combine with successive stages of the artist's manipulation (and, in a sense, the viewer's perception) of images; it is an accumulation of decisive but not definitive viewpoints which multiply and modify the limitless possibilities of the work in the random flow of time.

Rauschenberg's paintings are "celebrations of inconstancy" (to quote the artist's friend John Cage); they reverse the time-honoured relationship of trust

Robert Rauschenberg
(1925)
Factum II, 1957.
Combine painting on canvas.

between the viewer and the picture. The viewer is absorbed willy-nilly into a danger zone of treacherous reflections, pairings, simultaneous occurrences, explosions, and transparent layers (obtained by means of collage and various techniques of reproduction, mainly silkscreening), where familiar guideposts turn into traps. The eye is plunged into a maelstrom of active confusion; it is forced to abandon old habits of seeing and tries to adjust to the new forces animating reality.

Rauschenberg alters visual habits not by using the aggressive expressions and shock images that would later become the stock in trade of the second generation of Pop artists (Andy Warhol, Roy Lichtenstein, James Rosenquist), but by accepting the graceless, possibly pointless chaos of the world with an eye unprejudiced and almost impassive. What he succeeds in conveying (seemingly without trying to or even thinking about it) is the way reality comes into being; not just the signs and traces of outer reality—colours, forms, textures, and so forth—but the way things blush or burst into existence, the faint ring of phosphorescence that surrounds them as they surface in the present.

A Rauschenberg canvas is thus a very sensitive surface or screen on which reality deposits a film (like the misting of breath on a windowpane) consisting of indecipherable inscriptions, isolated letters, stray numbers, half erased faces, unused (and unusable) telephotographs, fresh (and already timeless) memories, senseless crimes, meaningless events. To this the artist may spontaneously add discarded objects, redundant materials, scraps of cloth and cardboard which just happened to be handy. No principle of order, no distinct preference, seems to organize this debris. The artist is almost non-existent; it is as if he had tossed the fragments together without looking. Nothing reveals his involvement in the picture except a few casual brushstrokes, splashes of colour that soon peter out in lazy dribbles. You cannot even infer a specific space or action in the work. The picture's sampling of objects and documents is seemingly haphazard; these miscellaneous items might have been drawn to the page or canvas by some indiscriminate magnetic force. They are stuck there, blurred under washes of colour. Planes overlap and intersect, scraps of visual information accumulate in transparent layers, suspended there in a meaningless limbo, never quite obliterating each other but nevertheless cancelling out any possibility of narrative continuity.

Factum II is a perfect example of this process: it thwarts your aesthetic judgment, as if the artist had finally reached the zero level of expressivity, a com-

plete absence of formal intention. Things appear and disappear for no visible reason. Nothing connects the fragments; they seem to be covered by a blanket of obliviousness, or a thin tulle which veils their possible coherence, the hidden continuity in their life. Their casual organization (or rather studied disorganization) proves nothing, asserts nothing. They are disconcertingly pointless. Rauschenberg's art urges us towards an awareness of emptiness, a "horizon of impossibility" (Alain Jouffroy). Not located in art or in reality, but in some intermediate "waiting" area (one of those grimly neutral waiting rooms where society's casualties stand in line), these works are oddly fascinating. Poised on the threshold of expression, they linger there, allowing the eye total freedom as they dawdle on the edge of choice and order.

COMBINING, RHYTHMIZING, CONSTRUCTING

It would be difficult to conceive of a position more opposed to the ideal of bringing art and life together than the one held by the painter Ad Reinhardt at the height of action painting and Pop Art. A lucid, ironically critical observer of the mundane dealings between artists and galleries, the confusions inherent in contemporary ideas about the social function of art, and the sentimental enthusiasms warping the pictorial truth of painting, Ad Reinhardt was an uncompromising champion of pure abstraction—of art-as-art as opposed to art confused with nature or perception or realism or existentialism: he was in fact the only member of the New York School to begin and end his career as an abstract artist.

But before producing his series of "uniform black square evanescences," as he described the monochrome works he painted from 1953 until his death ("ultimate paintings" from which texture, touch, form, colour, light, time, chance, movement—and of course collage—have been excised, they have no theme, contain no motifs, no symbols or signs, give "neither pleasure nor pain," and are the outcome of "neither insane work nor an insane avoidance of work"), Reinhardt had yielded towards the end of the thirties to the attractions of a style he characterized as "neo-classically manneristic post-Cubism" and had produced a number of collages which possess some of the richness and motility of visual reality.

Ad Reinhardt
(1913-1967)
Collage, 1939.
Pasted paper.

And notwithstanding the crisp outlines of the fragments Reinhardt scissors from magazines (which do
away with any randomness of line and colour resulting from the non-mechanical nature of his hand), and
notwithstanding the fact that the rigorous organization of forms is a response to his need to give the
picture surface an order whose only justification is its
absolute unity, his collages accommodate (though he
himself denies this) the rhythms of external reality.
The hectic throbbing of machines, the syncopations
of the street, the jumble of simultaneous impressions
which assail the city dweller from every direction—
they are all present in Reinhardt's work.

145

IN THE art of Ellsworth Kelly collage plays a leading part. It is a technique that this artist has employed again and again since 1950 when he discovered, in random arrangements of pasted papers, a basis for the experiments he was then conducting with abstract forms prior to transferring them to canvas.

As the title and state of preservation of this collage suggests, the act of cutting out and arranging independent paper fragments becomes the foundation for an architecture consisting of both solid and intensely coloured masses—an architecture which creates, with its simplified internal relationships, a perception of a monumental yet weightless space. As

in the work of Hans Arp (whose freely assembled compositions inspired by the ''laws of chance'' Kelly particularly admired), as in that of Henri Matisse (whose cutouts we are reminded of by Kelly's distinctive use of pure colours distributed in large flat areas), the picture surface in the American artist's work never lends itself to expressing a dramatic event or break. Kelly, who fully assimilated the teachings of his two forerunners, succeeds in freeing colour from the dictatorship of form, insofar as, in his works, colour actually becomes form, organizing space at will, modulating it with a naturalness and freedom from constraint that are totally convincing.

Ellsworth Kelly
(1923)
Study for Palisade, 1959.
Pasted paper.

Richard Diebenkorn
(1922)
Untitled No. 10, 1983.
Gouache, acrylic, crayon and pasted paper.

WITH the California artist Richard Diebenkorn, this sense of freedom is so great that it achieves a kind of transparency, a fluid interchange of inner and outer, a fusion of air and sea glimpsed through the frame of an open window—you get the impression that you are suspended in a no man's land between the two elements.

Here strips of pasted paper embedded in gouache or acrylic paint (sunk in colour, as it were) act less as an architectural foundation to the picture than as bits of film sensitive to the slightest nuances of an airy radiance. Their position on the optical watershed between depth and surface makes them analogous to the telltales on a sailboat, those gauzy ribbons attached to shrouds that signal the first tremulous breath of air on a windless sea. These hidden fragments, made perceptible by slight ripples on the pictorial surface, indicate a shifting space.

IT WAS in Florence during an extended visit to Italy, while looking through an antiquarian bookseller's portfolios, that William Dole discovered, in 1958, his personal version of the pasted paper technique. Browsing in that Arno-side bookstall, flicking through that miscellaneous collection of engraved plates and odd sheets bearing inscriptions or simple decorative motifs, he glimpsed new graphic possibilities for the modern artist.

After taking pages scissored from old books, tinted handmade sheets of paper, ruled invoice forms, bookbinding paper, and so forth, and then preparing them in a resourceful variety of ways (dipping them, brushing them, steeping them in different liquids, partly washing out the handwriting or print on them), Dole proceeded to cut them into fragments which he arranged on the picture surface, carefully respecting the spaces, breaks, or seams between them. He sought out and brought out harmonies between different materials, structures, forms, and hues.

In the result, beneath the grid of his airy, delicately constructed musical scores, you discern traces of colour, half-erased printed motifs, letters, numbers, designs, a few words in a foreign language, a truncated sentence or two; and these invite you to attempt a learned, discontinuous reading of the work. Space unfolds tortuously in these deftly contrived collages, with all the labyrinthine abstruseness of an alchemical treatise; tempting your eye and mind down misleading paths; confusing you with cross-references, subtle connections, occult allusions, enigmatic hints, secret formulae ; forcing you to construct a unity out of the extreme fragmentation of the mosaic-like image.

THE ORGANIZING principle underlying Robert Courtright's art is based on the art of building walls. Courses of small monochrome squares which seem to tremble in changing light record his impressions of Rome's medieval and Baroque façades. On his first visit in

William Dole
(1917-1983)
Ad Hoc, 1964.
Pasted paper.

1952, Courtright became fascinated by the way the Eternal City's buildings embrace different styles, periods, and materials quarried from older constructions. With its incrustations of miscellaneous ornaments alien to one another, its ancient inscriptions almost worn to illegibility or partly masked by the ex-votos of later centuries, its stuccos eaten away by the leprosy of dampness, its contrasting courses of travertine and brick, Rome's architecture is a real collage. A collage which not only animates and breaks up surfaces into variegated cells that reflect and refract a shifting, adaptable light, but bears witness also to a continuity that, by its very diversity, triumphs over all the turmoil and upheavals of history.

Courtright's method of making his pictures is, first of all, to prepare the papers he chooses according to thickness, weight, texture, softness or brittleness, and grain. Through a variety of treatments, such as dipping, dyeing, and scraping, he gives them a patina which partially erases their designs. Then he covers them with monochrome paint, allowing a ghostly image to show through here and there. Finally, he cuts these prepared sheets into small regular shapes, usually squares, which he glues to a support. The fragments are distributed in such a way that they respect the almost imperceptible nuances in their hues, the directions or grain of the brushstrokes, the accents and accidents resulting from random palimpsest effects.

The subtly modulated colours are enhanced by the infinitely sensitive play of light captured by the flakes and flukes caused by the natural shrinkage of the paper fragments, which alter our perception of the work at different times of the day, under different skies.

Thus the danger of monotony and austerity is obviated. Relieved of any onus that might have weighed them down, the isolated images drift in an indeterminate distance. They speak of Rome, but they also evoke the Apollonian grandeur of New York, where the artist lives during part of the year. As Matisse remarked, back in 1930, this kind of image stripped of its material nature and homogeneity resolves into an ecstatic iridescence through a play of light akin to that which produces, on a building's façade, "a gradation of tones evaporating into the sky as they take on the softness of the heavenly radiance" into which the architecture blends.

Antoni Tàpies
(1923)
Newspaper Cross, 1946-1947.
Pasted paper and ink.

TESTING TEXTURES

Now that the sheet of paper no longer served exclusively as the ground for line drawing and colouring, now that the tactile resources of its surface texture had begun to be exploited, first by the Cubists, then by the Futurists and the Constructivists, and then to unequalled effect by Kurt Schwitters, many painters of all tendencies took an interest in the optical combinations arising from different textures, coarse grained or fine, and from the varying thickness of the many kinds of paper available on the market.

Already in the mid-1920s an artist like Magnelli, in his abstract compositions, was getting remarkable effects of light and sensuousness by using industrial products like corrugated cardboard, canvas board, tarred and mottled papers, carbon and emery papers, and others imitating leather, sackcloth, wood-graining and so on.

Effects of contrast or tactile realism were the ones most commonly aimed at. But some artists, following the example set by Hans Arp, were more attracted by "metabolic" procedures, such as bring about the internal transformations of matter, such as may determine its alloys or its faculties of reaction in this or that situation.

Not content with simply taking the finished products, standard and calendered, of the paper industry, these men have an eye rather for the havoc that they can wreak on the very nature of paper, without bringing into play the classic instruments of the draughtsman or even the pair of scissors wielded by the cut-out artist. Yet the wounds of all sorts that these artists inflict on paper (for when they don't tear it up, they crumple or maculate it, they scratch it or slash it, they fold it, compress it, even burn it) serve in reality to set off its specific material properties, to bring out the artistic or inartistic qualities inherent in it, to retraverse the history of all the chemical or mechanical metamorphoses which the constituent substances have undergone, through dressing and priming, from the initial shredding and pounding and soaking to the final drying and coating.

Beginning as a malleable and receptive pulp, resulting from the cycle of destruction/recuperation/regeneration, paper is a living substance which, depending on the origin and structure of its component fibres and sizing, may lend itself to a variety of uses; indeed to as many and as delicately shaded variations as those which the sculptor obtains from the respective qualities of marble, granite, clay, plaster and so on. Not unlike hard or tender kinds of stone, dense or crumbly kinds of wood, certain papers are smooth or resistant, others rough to the touch, fluffy or silky, still others so fragile that they react to the least breath. Some papers absorb the artist's assault and seem to thrive on metamorphosis; others withstand it or yield to it and show off their gaping wounds.

It is a curious fact, or a natural consequence, that this new, ever keener interest in paper textures appeared just when the old papermills were going out of business, just when the chemical pulps which since the nineteenth century were replacing natural fibres and rags were proving to be dangerously unstable. So that a pervading nostalgia for better products disappearing from the market was implicitly combined with criticism of a society whose industrial output was now being regimented by the laws of the assembly line and standardization.

Instead of choosing his materials, Antoni Clavé prefers to be chosen by them. He depends on chance to bring them to hand. And his hand, docile and responsive, follows up the suggestions inscribed in their structure, much as a blind man's fingers identify an object by feeling their way over its uneven, refractory, broken or creviced surface. In the astonishing chaos of his reliefs, where the shattered fragments of a very thick white Arches paper still convey—despite a good deal of lacerating and grinding down—the impact of remote and silent stellar bombardments, the one guide offered to the questing sensibility is this caressing hand thanks to which any true craftsman recognizes the quality of a material. His eyes closed, he relies on his fingers alone. They evaluate the weight of the material, its density, texture and any flaws therein. Unfailingly they determine its duration and provenance. And from the intimate knowledge thus gained, he draws as with a much loved instrument a widening scale of unsuspected harmonies.

What at first glance distinguishes the pasted papers of Chillida is the way they occupy the sheet. Reaching out to the edges, or opening up richly satisfying gaps in the parts left intact, the scissored blocks recall the obsessive necessities of sculpture which compel the artist to set space adrift or shifting, to allow at all times for its action, which continually modifies, reverses or amplifies the relations between volumes.

These small compositions, apparently so simple, sober and rare, have the power of suggesting, at one glance, both the fullness of the sculpted work and its reduction to the plane surface. This impression (which is not easy to render in the photographic reproduction) is conveyed thanks to the extraordinary finesse with which Chillida handles and indeed exalts his materials.

The varying thickness of the paper, its grain and density, the orientation of the wire marks, the accidents that may have occurred during the manipulations which form its previous history, all this assumes a determining importance. Ink or paste stains, the trace of dirty or the bruise of rough fingers, greasiness or calcination, these are the equivalent here of the rust and corrosion on the sculptor's steel slabs, or of the veinings in the imposing mass of his wooden planks, the traces of formwork left on the sides of his concrete constructions, the translucent paleness of his alabasters.

On the model of his assemblages in space, the elements of cut-out paper are fitted together in a puzzle of ingenious and deceptive overlays whose pent-up energy is the result of a merciless struggle between tellingly devised cutouts and the luminous void which they surround. That void, swallowed up like an underlying outburst within and behind the cutouts, whistling over their edges, frays the sheet with a burning fire.

IT WAS again as a sculptor that the English artist Anthony Caro tested out the resources of pasted papers. By passing through the press various sheets of a heavy wove paper, he obtained a formidable energy contraction comparable in many ways to that suggested, rather threateningly, by his steel pieces. By making play all at once with foldings and tearings, with the resistential structure and malleability of the paper, he succeeded in expressing the elasticity characteristic of his material of predilection, which is progressively altered by the ensuing operations of compression, surfacing and crushing. As a finishing touch, the strokes of colour laid in with a deft brush over the bumpy surface foldings which set the light vibrating, in much the same way that polishing, soldering, and rusting come as a corrective to the roughness of the cut-out metal.

But the void that opens up between the creases created by the overlays and turnbacks of the paper, as also by the independent base which sets the composition in relief, invite the viewer to regard this work as an object in space, a sort of contemporary bas-relief rather than a pure product of the pasted paper technique.

MUCH the same may be said of Kenneth Noland's collage of 1980. Here again one meets with the effect of optical vibration resulting from the interaction of colours so characteristic of his art. Yet the working of the materials, the working of actual matter, seems in this case primordial, beginning with the choice of an uncalendered, unshaped paper which bears at every point the marks of its deeper, still uncouth nature.

Noland's first step with his material is to emphasize its power of absorption. The paper has not been touched or stained with colours, it has literally drunk them in;

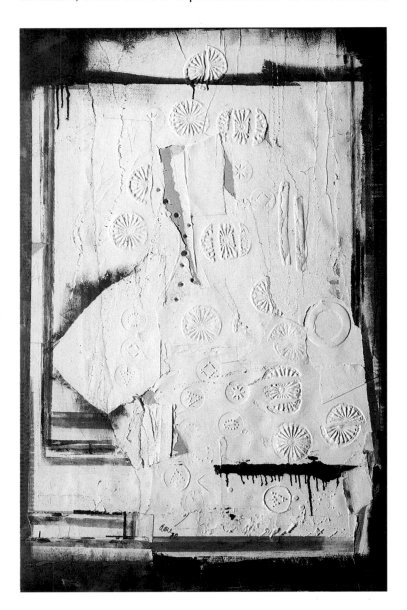

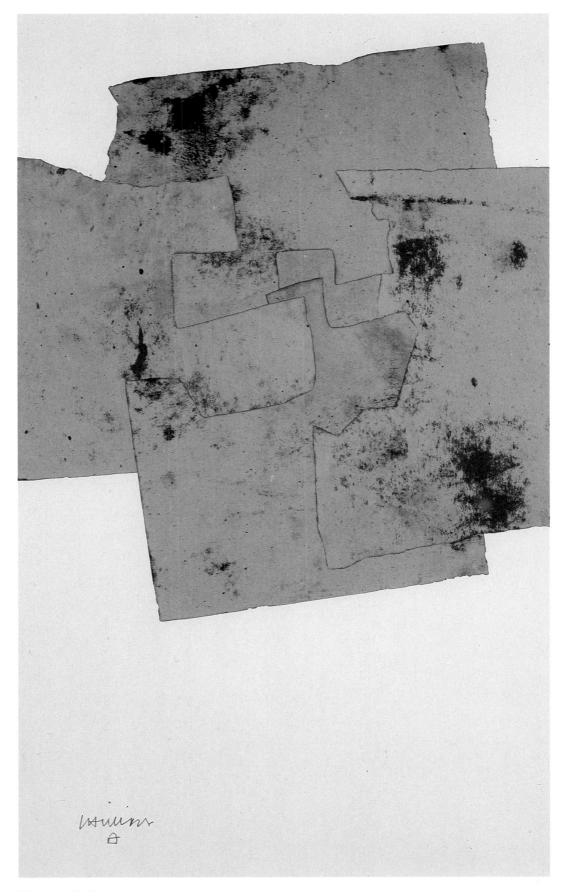

Eduardo Chillida
(1924)
Composition, 1963-1964.
Pasted paper.

◁ **Antoni Clavé**
(1913)
Stars in Relief, 1970.
Pasted paper and embossing.

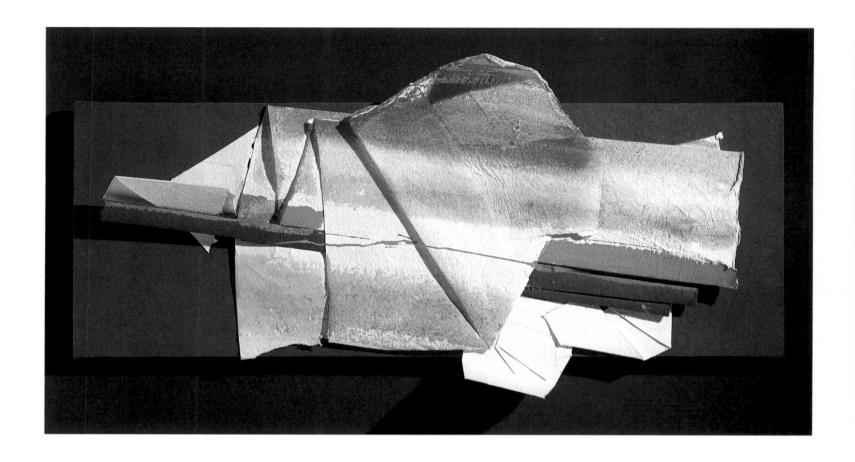

it has been gradually impregnated with their substance. Following up this passive, interiorizing movement, the further operations of drying, pressing, moulding, twisting, seem calculated to make the material disgorge the fragments thus pieced together, whose surface offers a rich display of plastic interactions continually catching and stimulating the eye. Now it is the inner texture of the materials which, rising like leavened dough, surges up and exhibits the eye-pleasing wealth of its chequered physical features, creating a dynamism of shadows and lights, of thicknesses and voids, of meditated slackenings which go to complete the game of assemblage.

A FEW pieces of torn paper (as elsewhere in the work of Tàpies a handful of sand, a few sticks of windblown straw caught up in the pulp, a couple of pink knots held by netting) have come this way by chance, or providentially, and got trapped in the sheet opposing its dark and compact block to the dispersion that prevails outside it.
Tokens of a brief flurry, these frail and tender scraps, still a-quiver from the winging flight that brought them here, roughly handled and barely held in place by a spot of paste, stand forth on the surface of the work as an unlooked-for testimony to the "destiny of the ephemeral." But at the same time their material

Anthony Caro
(1924)
Untitled, 1981.
Folded and gouache-painted paper
mounted on wood.

presence is quite unmistakable: dramatized by the light that plays over the accidented array of folds and tears, it points to a resistance, to something like a mute and nameless revolt, pent-up and held in by unseen walls, as of a prison or town.

Here, as almost always in the painting of Tàpies, two opposing movements are at work. On the one hand, the picture is that very partition or dividing wall which keeps any dispersion of sight from taking place, which rules out any trajectory of the eye that fails to go straight to the image as strictly defined by the sharp edges of the frame.

But, on the other hand, to this abstract area set up before us with the sudden violence of a lightning flash, are added and overlaid the accumulated records of lived experience, now painful, now joyful. Over the walls formed by the pictures of Tàpies, the chosen or random materials he deposits there mark out as many separations, cloisterings, and disjoinings as they do hopes and declarations of love. They gather into their thickness all the echoes of secret and clumsy speech, the wreckage of suffering, disgust, anger.

But the canvases of this ever inventive Spanish artist receive into themselves too all the metamorphoses that nature, changing seasons, and changing weathers slowly and secretly impose on the order of the visible world. Those metamorphoses are the memory of that visible order—a memory which harbours the outcries and wounds, the parchings of the sun, the frosts of winter, and the upcomings of sap and seed.

Kenneth Noland
(1924)
PR-08-80, 1980.
Collage of tinted papers.

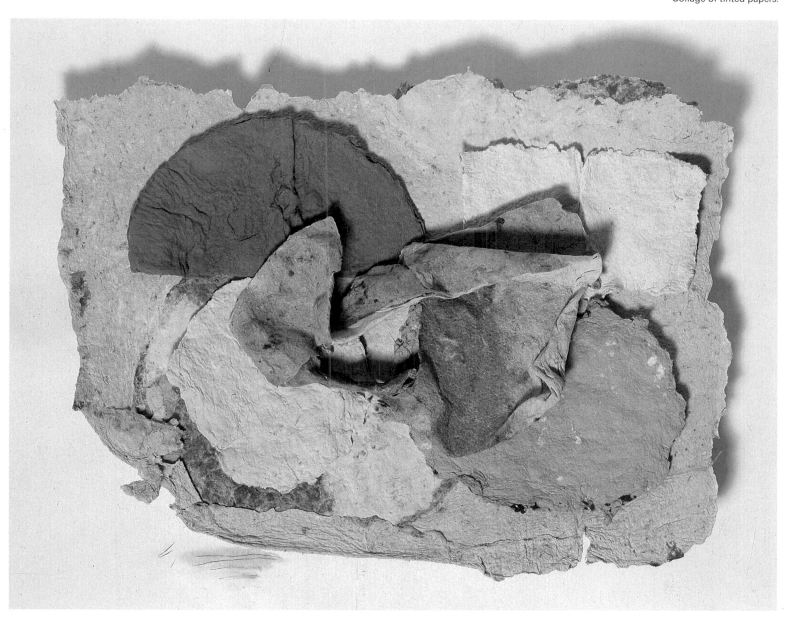

Jiri Kolar
(1914)
Death of the Diplomat, 1970.
Chiasmage.

ACCUMULATING, SATURATING, DENOUNCING ENTROPY

FAR REMOVED from the kind of reverie on materials that lingers lovingly on the substance of the paper and the effects produced upon it by the action of outside forces, a number of artists, less nostalgic perhaps, but no less sensual or anxious, began to explore a realm of images chosen deliberately from among the most trivial of those produced by the new illustration industry. With frankness and determination, they undertook to question and then to exploit certain previously unused aspects which had come into being in those years through the amazing development of image reproduction techniques: for example, the exaggerated repetition of a single motif, increasingly disorganized associations of extremes of all kinds and the resulting debasement of meaning. Many began cutting up magazines—contemporary ones this time, without the amusing incongruities offered by the old-fashioned vignettes of Max Ernst. Scientific periodicals, cookery and nature magazines with their tantalizing colour spreads, industrial catalogues, fashion magazines, luxurious art books, young people's encyclopaedias and comic books were the sources from which these artists culled a wide-ranging repertory of motifs which they then disposed on their canvases in repetitive figures, with artful juxtapositions and redundancies, until the eye, saturated by so many visual suggestions, and lacking a firm foundation, experiences a violent nausea.

This queasiness, however, is due less to the subject presented than to the very nature of the material being used, the pseudo-verity which it cynically transmits on glossy paper. It is the affiliation of these ever-smiling images to the realm of mass reproductibility that creates the accumulative obsession of these works; it is the anarchic juxtaposition of information relentlessly thrown onto the page or screen that dictates the plethoric manner of artists like Erró and Kolar. The society in which these painters live is ruled by film and printed matter, and their own devouring urgency forces perception to make an ever more limited selection, sacrificing the complex truth of beings and events to the imperious simplification of immediate effects in which all messages that are not directly effective are condemned sooner or later to oblivion. In this shopwindow vision of reality, manifested at the time by the appearance of the fabulous world of the supermarket, shadows are eliminated by a cold, insistent light, and a deliberate dramatization abolishes the space that ordinarily surrounds objects; where the superfluous is king, hasty formulations serve as conclusions, and the density of language is reduced to the polite platitudes of the cliché.

In the same way, the frenetic production of information and images continually disseminated by the mass media obliterates all differences: they play with time and space, passing incontinently from the authentic to the fake, from seriousness to levity, and so all values are reduced to a mean that finally becomes undistinguishable from the void. From then on, in the midst of this undifferentiated disorder, devoid of quality and hope, the gruesome stands side by side with the delectable, and the genius of the race-horse, not to say of a laundry detergent, as Robert Musil had already foreseen in 1920, vies with the most daring productions of the human spirit and the emotions filtered by the poet's art. Politics, sex, science, and entertainment, all are on the same level: the sheer number of texts finally makes reading impossible, in every corner of the globe creature comforts ease the difficulties and surprises that were once the charm of travel; all desires seem ludicrous when the extremes of life become the object, among so many others, of superficial talk exchanged in pleasant company.

Art, as the final refuge of a voice that can both ensure and increase exchanges between individuals and the world, is especially threatened by this devaluation of meaning—which also coincided with the sudden inflation in the prices for art works. The mass reproduction of works of universal culture tends to defuse irrevocably the surprise that should accompany their discovery; in separating paintings, frescoes, and architecture from their usual context and function, photographic reproductions dispense the eye from a contact with the subtleties of materials, the particularities of a geography, the requirements of a cult. And when it is not the analyses of specialists that render the content of a work inaccessible to sincere and immediate emotion, the exploitation of their motifs for advertising purposes saps the power of these images to the point of reducing them to plain, lifeless signs easily replaceable by any other element of communication.

157

IT TOOK the robust vitality of the Icelandic artist Erró for the entropic menace and the formal depreciation that hangs over contemporary imagery to be attacked head on and with equal arms.

It is safe to say that no one else today possesses to the same degree as Erró the power to give the trivial and the overdone an epic and magical dimension; and although it seems as if he were leaving the initiative to the apparently inexpressive images of others, without inventing any figures of his own, he displays an exceptional gift for orchestration which he uses to harmonize contrary proportions, or to play on their contrast, to accentuate a particular part of the composition, to heighten certain graphic effects, or, in other cases, to divide the surface into a number of clearly distinct planes, or to fill it entirely with a single repetitive motif, like an orchestral tutti.

His collages, which match the scale and serial principles of industrial production, collect the anarchic profusion of objects, figures, and styles drawn from among the illustrated publications of all kinds that flood the newsstands and bookshops. Not only do they exploit and harp on the inevitable juxtapositions that such an overabundance of images creates, but they further emphasize the disorder and brutality of the oppositions: thanks to his corrosive sense of humour and inexhaustible imagination, constantly stimulated by the promptings of chance, thanks, especially, to a supremely developed sense of analogy and potential associations suggested by the style and themes of his sources, his work presents multiple facets.

What he gives us to see can be interpreted as the unfettered transcription of a certain rage to live, an evident pleasure in abandoning himself to the whirlwind of the present, or as a burlesque denunciation of the violence and frenzy festering worldwide in the totalitarian regimes or in the societies satisfied with the illusions procured by an outrageous opulence.

The paintings that Erró first made after these early montages of illustrations all present a very careful execution, the paint forming a thin, lacquer-like surface that neutralizes the material and stylistic differences between the various models in their original state; there is also a sort of frosty light that gives a neutral, even value to all the elements of the composition, freezing the objects into the fixity, one is tempted to say, of a shopwindow.

Adding humour to his unquenchable curiosity, and with the boisterous joy that characterizes him, the Icelandic artist blithely combines Old Master nudes and space-age heroes, not hesitating to place the likenesses of famous men, politicians, painters, and musicians, in the company of brawling cowboys and invaders from outer space.

And yet, however unbridled the energy of the forms hurtling across these canvases may seem—weapons and engines spewing streaks of flame, avenging riders dashing across the foreground, bodies thrashing in erotic or intergalactic combat—these forms soon resolve into a perfect pictorial equanimity that renders credible and even natural the most outlandish encounters, and which completely de-realizes the veracity of details lost in the enormity of an encyclopaedic and totalizing vision.

In the series of colossal panoramic landscapes, like the *Planescape* of 1972, the absurd accumulation of objects indiscriminately piled together results in the abolition of all meaning or spatial legibility. The sheer excess and endless repetition of these motifs leads to the consciousness of a void: faced with the invasion of ever the same thing, all that remains is the stupefied

Jiri Kolar
(1914)
Visual Poetry, 1963.
Collage.

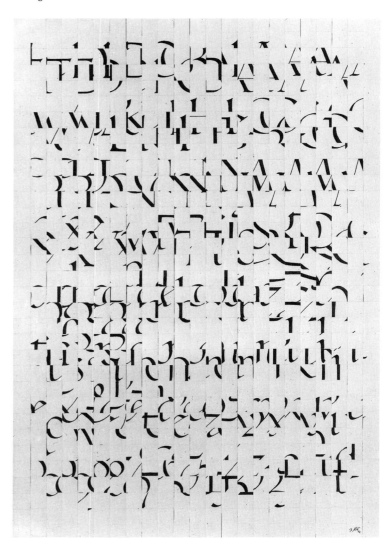

Erró
(1932)
Planescape, 1972.
Collage of illustrations.

contemplation of a world caught in an irreversible process of glaciation; fuselages, wings, and motors fossilizing into a fatal immobility.

No SOONER had Jiri Kolar experienced the power of words as a poet than he became aware of their profoundly, intrinsically rebellious nature. Instead of bringing unity and appeasement, they were, in his eyes, a constant source of misunderstanding, strife, and anguish, always leading to an impasse; instead of being durable and resplendent with the compact order of their mission, they displayed their deficiencies and ragged condition. And the greater their number, the more frequently and loudly they were intoned, the more their prestige seemed to decline. This is why, n 1938, Kolar decided to combat the lies and indigence that menace today's cultures based on the written word; by subjecting the triteness and smugness of moronic messages to a meticulous and systemat c

sabotage capable of restoring the free and natural respiraticn of speech to the printed text, beyond the uncontrolled—or perhaps skilfully maintained—confusion.

By all sorts of experiments on words as a formal material, the Czech artist strove to tear down the authoritative structures of explanatory discourse, in order to distil its purely visual music. A virtuoso of the scissors, he gradually divested letters, words and phrases of their original and principal function: to translate a concept or to bring a line of reasoning to its conclusion. Violating the militaristic rigour of typographic order, deserting the columns and soon the page itself, these fragments of exploded text attained free space: there, as hieroglyphs without an Egypt, floating writing without a support, they offer a new reading of reality, an equivocal reading, indeed, because it is on the borderline between word and image.

The same voluntary ambiguity led to the numerous visual "figures of speech" that Kolar invented one after the other in the late fifties. These were originally syntactical manipulations intended to save from banalization by mass reproduction images which a few short years before had been rare and venerated, but were then being pressed into every kind of service. Slicing precisely into the over-connoted tissue of idols of popularized art such as Raphael, Botticelli, Ingres, Bruegel, and Bosch, to mention just these few, Kolar operated like a mischievous surgeon to make all sorts of transplants, amputations, permutations, larvae, and chrysalides, through which his unbounded imagination mocked habitual perception and strove to heighten or accelerate the inner faculties of the eye.

In what he called his "rollages" or "cubomanias," he cut out images and redistributed and pasted them so that the paper surface seems to multiply, scatter, and spread in all directions, as if it had been recombined by a prism. In another technique called "crumplage" (from the verb crumple), he subjected the flaunted figures of classical painting to horrible torments and deformations which, however, were meant to renew their energy, to regenerate the vitality lost in the reproduction process. In his "intercollages" especially, meaning is constantly mirrored by unpredictable rebounds of the memory and all sorts of allusive enigmas facilitated by the formal and iconographic juxtapositions in which the artist liked to indulge.

But it is probably the "chiasmages" (a term derived from the criss-cross shape of the Greek letter *chi*) which best express the dual sensitivity of this artist who was both a poet and an image-maker. In the many works produced by this principle, like the *Death of the Diplomat* of 1970 (page 156), the little pieces of paper torn from the pages of a book regain, by their interweaving pattern, a visual function that is other than explicative or enumerative: the text once again becomes texture, the outer envelope of idea and emotion. The invention of the "chiasmage" thus seems to demand that writing become a dead letter, an obsolete and broken message, before recovering the original virtue that it had in all civilizations based on the Book, i.e., to start weaving around things an intelligible and light material, sufficiently tight to protect them, but loose enough to let the beauty of a spiritual essence show through the texture of a pure musical respiration.

BUT THERE is not the least possibility of any escape for space in the *Reliquaries of Chosen Papers* by Bernard Réquichot, nor the least hope that the eye can avoid being overwhelmed by the chaos of coloured shapes, by the slow, repeated fall of these cut-out forms, among which may be recognized the equivocal details of a reality reproduced by an eye-catching advertisement: in this case, the sickening dispersion of a table overflowing with food. And even though it is true that, as Réquichot himself remarked, "the assemblage, fragmentation, and superposition of the pieces are made according to affinities of colour, luminosity or visual rhythm, such that a new image replaces the original images, each of which is also transformed," the sheer abundance of these fragments collected at the bottom of this precious casket, profane relics, paper debris curling into spirals for lack of space, in fact results in complete illegibility. The insane, useless content of these images is nothing more than the deluxe dumping ground of a religion devoted to the worship and enjoyment of the ephemeral, a hall of mirrors in which are reflected *ad infinitum* the deceptions of a macabre vanity. As with Erró, but this time with a sentiment of dramatic impotence and stifled revolt, the saturation produced by cut and pasted accumulations denounces the equivalence of diversity and sameness, the silent, indifferent identity of fullness and emptiness.

Each of Réquichot's striking, tension-filled works manifests a desperate effort to escape from the ineluctable encirclement, the ever-increasing asphyxiation to which consumer society, with its industries of knowledge and sensation, condemns all true emotion, any truly authentic voice. Thus the spiral, an essential and recurrent theme in Réquichot's work, seems to represent the headlong flight that eventually led the artist to make his tragic leap into the unknown on December 4, 1961; and yet, although the movement of this form represents the invariable return of the same, it also holds within it the hope of someday overcoming the obstacle of repetition and death. This is also why the letters that Réquichot left behind on the eve of his suicide, though undecipherable, contain the promise of a correspondence that will finally be fulfilled and shared, the content and questions of which will become one with the pure vibrations of writing or speech.

Bernard Réquichot
(1929-1961)
Reliquary of Chosen Papers, 1961.
Magazine illustrations cut out
and pasted on canvas.

The pasted paper, under its many different aspects, stands out as the most poetic and revolutionary moment in the evolution of painting, the touching take-off point towards some more reliable assumptions, a closer intimacy with everyday truths, the invincible affirmation of the provisional and of timebound and perishable materials, and the sovereignty of thought.

Tristan Tzara

SEAMARKS

THIS appropriation of art by high finance and the mass media, towards meretricious ends unrelated to its own, led a large number of the younger artists in the mid-sixties to shun the official art circuit and to develop an underground, transitory, intentionally enigmatic activity capable of restoring the eye to its original condition as a hunter, a roving seeker out of sensations, receptive to any stimuli that may be encountered.

But even then the question arose and had to be faced: how to capture the vital energy of vision itself, at the very instant that it makes its awesome appearance on the retina, before words and projects take hold of it and begin to brake its momentum?

Although all too keenly aware of the impossibility of innocence in a world of overwhelming material values, the European and American artists who in those years belonged to movements as diverse as Fluxus, Neo-Dada or Conceptual Art, all wanted to resuscitate the type of wonder experienced by the early explorers who in their travels stumbled across entire forgotten civilizations or monuments buried in the depths of time, the unexpected beauty of which was enhanced by their utter abandonment and by the fact that their meaning and function remained inaccessible to understanding, however cunningly brought to bear.

At the same time as the unknown parts of the planet shrink further each day with the encroachments of science, technology, and tourism, artists on all sides are creating works that present dreams of virgin territories, precolumbian Americas, and mythical cities barely emerged from their ashes; miniature ruins, simple forms dug out of the ground, washed up objects and debris today constitute the traces of a past which the eye must learn to decipher; mysterious inscriptions, illegible for the most part, messages without a destination reinvent the treasure hunt, lead the eye onto the path of an inner jungle that has yet to be domesticated. Whether minute or monumental, ephemeral or defying eternity, these works placed off the beaten track, or, incongruously, at the very heart of the banal, raise the question of the still possible resurgence of the sacred.

Other artists using perishable materials, subject to the cycles of organic and physical transformations—ice, fire, lightning, plants—re-establish a connection with basic experiences that are too often scorned in our day. Finally, the creation of private, derisory events, whose incidental material vanishes at the very instant that it comes into being, the happenings and performances of all stripes, denounce the nightmare of History and try to oppose by minuscule displacements, barely perceptible deflections, the insidious threat of entropy that hangs over each of us and our environment. This minimal activity defines the limits of a back-country whose future is already in ruin, the flickering marks of a mythic time in which the immobile splendours of the Golden Age would have been replaced by the fluid drift of exploded moments destined to dissolve in non-fixity.

It is to seamarks such as these, perceived on the remotest shores of expression, that the eye clings when presented with the recent pasted paper works of artists belonging to this new sensitivity. They are almost always small, fragile compositions, with very little preparation, assembling on a sheet of paper a few elements from the artist's life or related to his current work, the relic or token of an entirely private event, without a future, the contents of a pocket, a travel souvenir, the traces of an occasion devoid of any particular significance, but which, in being brought together, dated, and eventually exhibited, should give the spectator the feeling of time preserved, of a precious glimmer rescued from the boredom of our lives and arts, from the uniformization of our attitudes towards life and art.

The elements that compose these works are not the product of chance, they do not contribute to the creation of a found object in the manner of the Surrealists. No, their association depends upon a deliberate choice made by the artist, who used them according to criteria known only to himself. The work of collage —which is not indispensable to the artistic comprehension of the work—resurrects the inoffensive magic of the nineteenth-century ex-votos, the fabrication of power objects and fetishes. But now the spell is no longer addressed to the past; what is evoked by these pasted paper works is reality itself, which now manifests itself only by these humble, discreet disruptions in the order of the visible, silent crystallizations of vision and memory, little monuments

Cy Twombly
(1929)
Untitled, 1959.
Torn and pasted paper.

raised apart, without a base, to the glory of the evanescent, gratuitous signs thanks to which, by dint of dispersion and dereliction, the eye may connect once again with the universal.

Over a sheet from a schoolboy's exercise book (or maybe from a writing pad) have been scattered some scraps of torn paper, like so many pebbles marking a trail, one that presumably leads back through the gates of childhood. In spite of the bewildering disorder, an inexplicable rightness makes itself felt in this uncomposed scattering, not only because of the imperceptible vibration of space arising from it, but also because the viewer is inescapably made to feel that here, in this apparently wanton marshalling of paltry, ill-treated materials, lies the key to a mysterious, long-sought destiny that the image at once invites us to grasp. Yielding to this appeal, the eye attempts to piece together a disrupted world on the strength of these barely visible traces, jumbled by loss of memory; or on the strength, it may be, of these trifling signs too soon abandoned by a baffled will. But the attempt cannot be carried through. The work holds its own, requiring to be seized in the expense of pure energy which its enigma calls forth. It is a transit, not a destination, a passing show, a flashing forth which soon lapses into non-fixity, sinking away in the shipwreck of our attention.

A familiar experience in Cy Twombly's painting, these pale anonymous signals, these illegible letters of a handwriting feverishly scrawled over the walls, this spontaneous and ciphered calligraphy embodying man's ancient, ever stirring urge to express his vitality, whether joy or terror, revolt or longing. In fact these imprints or gashes inflicted on the surface of the sheet are so many signposts set up to help the wandering eye on its way, to shepherd it and keep it going on its uncertain quest.

So it is that the charm of this work lies in its oscillation between memory and adventure, its reliance on nostalgia to shape and reshape its desire.

WHAT the recent collages of the Italian painter Nicola De Maria convincingly show is this: that the work is no longer meant to follow up a thesis, borne out by the strict limits of a frame or by the virtues of a particular technique; that it moves according to the whims of an untrammelled time-pattern which fluctuates with some precision. These scanty odds and ends, mere driftwood washed ashore here, which some nameless urge has brought together higgledy-piggledy, yet hold the eye, creating a new necessity which lies less in deciphering the riddle proposed by the image than in drifting with it on whatever its destined course may be. Looked at openmindedly, each accident of the paper, each spot of colour, each disclosure of texture, whether dense or meagre, regains a certain power of suggestion. The noble ruggedness of the cardboard, its rents and tears, tell of stubborn fighting; its lightness set off by a milky white, of storms weathered and left behind. The sheet torn out of a notebook tells on the contrary of a personal destiny, the painter's, confronted in the studio day after day by the unforgiving unit of the page, into which he pours little by little his misgivings and hopes, his failures and victories. The painted composition which goes to complete the image thus finds itself enshrined—like a new icon, but a precarious one, buffeted as it were by waves—between the margins of an ill-adjusted frame which, far from adding, detracts from its éclat; detracts from it by associating it with the occasions, even insignificant, even adverse occasions, involving setbacks and rebuffs, which have contributed to its birth and to such accidents of chance as may have deflected its trajectory towards other destinations.

Nicola De Maria
(1954)
Desire Removed (Desiderio Allontanato),
1977-1983.
Mixed media.

IT WAS not for the sake of encyclopaedic learning that, around 1970, Joseph Beuys brought together several admirable plates from a herbal, from which this *Pittosporum* was detached. He had no thought of gaining knowledge or constituting an epitome. What he wanted was to hark back to the outcome of a form, and to all that in its bare appearance it might contain in the way of mythical riches, collective memories and personal emotions. The point was to choose, perhaps to rescue, some of those tiny but decisive moments when the eye sees things in a new light, when from behind the veil emerge that freshness and simplicity with which the world in its totality can sometimes, in moments of vision, be perceived.

What in reality lies behind this frail idol with a Latin name which the artist has deposited so deftly on a makeshift support? Whence comes our response of pleasure and surprise at the sight of this unpretending image? Is it the contrast of the perfect form emitting its luminous exclamation on the rough surface of a piece of patched up cardboard? Is it the opposition between the fullness of ever green nature and the world of manufactured products subject to rough handling and steady wear and tear? True enough, part of our emotion arises from the implicit duality that balances this collage, as in part it also springs from the warmth of textures and colouring which set the mind dreaming of some other place where endless summer reigns. And yet, beyond the admirable plastic presence of this work, there stands the primary need to set some store by a thing which, at first sight, is hardly worth it. So it is that, for this poet and adventurer, this curious explorer of small opportunities met by the way or opening casually in the tissue of dream or memory, collage simply means *making visible*. The frailness carefully shepherded here by Beuys thus links up with those paltry offerings, paltry but ever so solacing because useless and irrelevant, which children and primitives make. Fetish objects, hastily thrown together from any bric-a-brac to hand, whose inexpressible value rests on no aesthetic judgment, on no sanction of history or custom, but on the love-token finally proffered when reason can no longer cope with the matter. In their sublime modesty, these stealthy guide-marks are offered merely as clues to the enigma of the visible, as in fact one artist's demonstration that painting shall remain, first and foremost, what one most wishes it to be: a gift.

Joseph Beuys
(1921-1986)
Pittosporum, 1970.
Collage.

BIBLIOGRAPHY

INDEX

LIST OF ILLUSTRATIONS

BIBLIOGRAPHY

General

Dawn ADES, *Photomontage*, Pantheon Books, New York 1967. — Louis ARAGON, *Les Collages*, Hermann, Paris 1965. — *The Art of Assemblage*, exhibition catalogue, Museum of Modern Art, New York 1961, text by W. Seitz. — E. BIESALSKI, *Scherenschnitt und Schattenrisse, kleine Geschichte der Silhouettenkunst*, Callwey, Munich 1964. — Rudi BLESH and Harriet JANIS, *Collage, Personalities, Concepts, Techniques*, Chilton Book Co., Philadelphia, New York, London 1967. — Arlette BUCHMAN and Victor D'AMICO, *Assemblage, A New Dimension in Creative Teaching*, Museum of Modern Art, New York 1972. — *Collagen aus sechs Jahrzehnten*, Frankfurter Kunstverein, Frankfurt am Main 1968, text by E. Rathke. — *Collagen*, exhibition catalogue, Kunstgewerbemuseum, Zürich 1968, 2 vols., text by E. Billeter. — *Collage et montage au théâtre et dans les autres arts*, L'Age d'Homme, Lausanne 1978. — *Collagen, Materialbilder, Objekte*. Kunstamt Wedding, Berlin 1982, text by L. Fischer. — *Collage*, exhibition catalogue, Kunsthaus, Zug (Switzerland) 1986. — John and Joan DIGBY, *The Collage Handbook*, Thames and Hudson, London 1985. — Philippe DUBOIS, *Le Collage*, Centre National de Documentation Pédagogique, Paris 1978. — Helen HUTTON, *The Technique of Assemblage*, London and New York 1968. — Ferit ISCAN, *Comment composer un tableau par collage, assemblage et relief*, Bordas, Paris 1985. — Norman LALIBERTÉ and Alex MOGELON, *Collage, Montage, Assemblage, History of Contemporary Techniques*, Van Nostrand Reinhold, New York 1974. — Dona MEILACH and Elvie TEN HOOR, *Collage and Found Art*, Reinhold Publishing Corporation, New York 1964 (Art Horizons, Inc.). — Herta WESCHER, *Die Collage*, Dumont, Cologne 1968; new edition under the title *Die Geschichte der Collage*, 1980; in English, *Collage*, translated by R.E. Wolf, Abrams, New York 1968. — Eddie WOLFRAM, *History of Collage, An Anthology of Collage, Assemblage and Events Structures*, Studio Vista, London 1975.

Studies and Monographs

Götz ADRIANI, *Robert Rauschenberg, Zeichnungen, Gouachen, Collagen 1949-1979*, Piper, Munich and Zürich 1980. — Guillaume APOLLINAIRE, *Les peintres cubistes*, Hermann, Paris 1965; *The Cubist Painters*, translated by Lionel Abel, Wittenborn, Schultz, New York 1949. — *Arp, le temps des papiers déchirés*, exhibition catalogue, Centre Georges Pompidou, Paris 1983, texts by P. Bruguière and C. Derouet. — Hans ARP and El LISSITZKY, *Die Kunstismen — Les Ismes de l'Art — The Isms of Art*, Zürich 1925. — *Art of This Century, Objects, Drawings, Photographs, Paintings, Sculpture, Collage, 1910 to 1942*, Peggy Guggenheim, Arno Press reprint, New York n.d. — *Autour d'André Breton*, exhibition catalogue, Artcurial, Paris 1986, text by J. Pierre. — *Autres Dimensions*, exhibition catalogue, Galerie Beyeler, Basel 1976. — *L'avant-garde au féminin*, exhibition catalogue, Artcurial, Paris 1984. — Joseph Beuys, *Dibujos — Drawings*, exhibition catalogue, Fundación Caja de Pensiones, Madrid 1985, text by H. Bastian. — Maria L. BORRÀS, *Picabia*, Albin

Michel, Paris 1985. — *Georges Braque, les papiers collés*, exhibition catalogue, Centre Georges Pompidou, Paris 1982, texts by D. Cooper, P. Daix, E. Fry, I. Monod-Fontaine, A. Martin and E.A. Carmen Jr. — André BRETON, *Le Surréalisme et la Peinture*, Gallimard, Paris 1928. — André BRETON, *Genèse et perspective artistiques du Surréalisme*, Paris 1941. — *Cinquante ans de collages*, exhibition catalogue, Musée d'Art et d'Industrie, Saint-Etienne 1964, texts by H. Wescher and M. Allemand. — *1910-1945 Collages and Reliefs*, exhibition catalogue, Annely Juda Fine Art, London 1982, text by J. Beckett. — *Collage*, exhibition catalogue, Galeria Joan Prats, Barcelona 1985. — *Dada-Constructivism, The Janus Face of the Twenties*, Annely Juda Fine Art, London 1984, texts by D. Ades, M. Dachy, P. de Haas, A. Nakov and R. Shepperd. — Pierre DAIX, *Le Cubisme de Picasso*, Ides et Calendes, Neuchâtel (Switzerland) 1979; *Picasso: The Cubist Years, 1907-1916*, Boston 1979. — Robert L. DELEVOY, *Dimensions du XXe siècle*, Skira, Geneva 1965; *Dimensions of the 20th Century*, Skira, New York 1965. — Marcel DUCHAMP, *Marchand du sel*, Le Terrain Vague, Paris 1958; reprinted under the title *Duchamp du signe. Ecrits*, Flammarion, Paris 1975. — *Dufrêne, Hains, Rotella, Villeglé, Vostell*, exhibition catalogue, Staatsgalerie, Stuttgart 1971. — Jacques DUPIN, *Joan Miró*, Flammarion, Paris 1961; *Joan Miró: Life and Work*, Abrams, New York 1962. — Jacques DUPIN, *L'espace autrement dit*, Galilée, Paris 1982. — John ELDERFIELD, *The Cut-Outs of Henri Matisse*, New York and London 1978. — John ELDERFIELD, *Kurt Schwitters*, Thames and Hudson, London 1985. — Max ERNST, *Ecritures*, Gallimard, Paris 1970. — *The Essential Cubism 1907-1920*, exhibition catalogue, Tate Gallery, London 1983, texts by D. Cooper and G. Tinterow. — *Estève*, exhibition catalogue, Galerie Claude Bernard, Paris 1974, text by J. Leymarie. — *Futurismo e Futurismi*, exhibition catalogue, Palazzo Grassi, Venice 1986. — *The Golden Age of Collage*, exhibition catalogue, Mayor Gallery, London 1987, text by T. Baum. — John GOLDING, *Cubism: A History and an Analysis 1907-1914*, London and New York 1959; new edition, 1968. — *Juan Gris*, exhibition catalogue, Madrid 1985, text by L. Kachur. — Wieland HERZFELDE, *John Heartfield, Leben und Werk*, VEB Verlag der Kunst, Leipzig 1962. — *Victor Hugo, soleil d'encre*, exhibition catalogue, Musée du Petit Palais, Paris 1985. — Alain JOUFFROY, *Une révolution du regard*, Gallimard, Paris 1964. — D.H. KAHNWEILER, *Juan Gris, sa vie, son œuvre, ses écrits*, Gallimard, Paris 1946. — *Jiri Kolar*, exhibition catalogue, Solomon R. Guggenheim Museum, New York 1975, text by T.M. Messer. — *Henri Laurens*, exhibition catalogue, Centre Georges Pompidou, Paris 1985, text by I. Monod-Fontaine. — Edward LUCIE-SMITH, *Art Now, From Abstract Expressionism to Superrealism*, New York and London 1977. — *Magnelli, ardoises et collages*, exhibition catalogue, Centre Georges Pompidou, Paris 1986, text by G.C. Argan. — MAN RAY, *Self-Portrait*, Boston 1963. — Henri MATISSE, *Ecrits et propos sur l'art*, edited by Dominique Fourcade, Hermann, Paris 1972. — *Matisse on Art*, edited by Jack D. Flam, Phaidon, London and Praeger, New York 1973. — *Mesens, 125 collages et objets*, exhibition catalogue, Knokke-le-Zoute 1963, text by J. Brunius. — *The Collage of Robert Mother-*

well, exhibition catalogue, Museum of Fine Arts, Houston 1972-1973. – Andrei NAKOV, *Abstrait-Concret, Art non objectif russe et polonais*, transédition, Paris 1981. – *Paris-Berlin, 1900-1933*, exhibition catalogue, Centre Georges Pompidou, Paris 1978. – Jean PAULHAN, *La peinture cubiste*, Denoël-Gonthier, Paris 1960. – Gaëtan PICON, *Journal du Surréalisme*, Skira, Geneva 1976; *Surrealism*, Skira, New York and London 1976, new edition 1983. – *The Planar Dimension, Europe 1919-1932*, exhibition catalogue, Solomon R. Guggenheim Museum, New York 1979, text by M. Rowell. – Jacques PRÉVERT, *Collages de Prévert*, Gallimard, Paris 1982. – *Robert Rauschenberg, Werke 1950-1980*, exhibition catalogue, Staatliche Kunsthalle, Berlin 1980. – *Bernard Réquichot*, exhibition catalogue, Centre National d'Art Contemporain, Paris 1973. – Hans RICHTER, *Dada: Art and Anti-Art*, McGraw-Hill, New York, and Thames and Hudson, London 1966. – *François Rouan*, exhibition catalogue, Centre Georges Pompidou, Paris 1983, texts by H. Damis, D. Bozo and I. Monod-Fontaine. – William RUBIN, *Dada and Surrealist Art*, Abrams, New York 1968. – Werner SCHMALENBACH, *Kurt Schwitters*, Dumont, Cologne 1967. – Pierre SCHNEIDER, *Matisse*, Flammarion, Paris and Rizzoli, New York 1984. – Arturo SCHWARZ, *New York Dada*, Prestel, Munich 1974. – *Silhouettes et découpures genevoises des XVIIIe et XIXe siècles*, exhibition catalogue, Musée d'Art et d'Histoire, Geneva 1985, texts by G. Apgar and A. de Herdt. – Werner SPIES, *Max Ernst, les collages, inventaires et contradictions*, Gallimard, Paris 1985. – Michel THÉVOZ, *Dubuffet*, Skira, Geneva 1986. – *Twelve American Masters of Collage*, exhibition catalogue, Andrew Crispo Gallery, New York 1977. – *The Twenties in Berlin: Baader, Grosz, Hausmann, Höch*, exhibition catalogue, Annely Juda Fine Art, London 1978-1979. – Tristan TZARA, *Œuvres complètes*, Flammarion, Paris 1980. – *Zeichnungen und Collagen des Kubismus: Picasso, Braque, Gris*, exhibition catalogue, Kunsthalle, Bielefeld 1979.

Essays and Articles

Louis ARAGON, "La peinture au défi," catalogue preface, collage exhibition, Galerie Goemans, Paris, March 1930. – Tristan TZARA, "Le papier collé ou le proverbe en peinture," *Cahiers d'Art*, No. 2, Paris 1931. – *Art d'aujourd'hui*, special issue on collage, Paris, March-April 1954. – "Les papiers collés du Cubisme à nos jours," *XXe Siècle*, No. 6, Paris, January 1956. – Clement GREENBERG, "The Pasted-Paper Revolution," *Art News*, New York, September 1958. – Jean PAULHAN, "L'espace cubiste ou le papier collé," *L'Arc*, No. 10, Paris 1960. – Robert ROSENBLUM, "Picasso and the Coronation of Alexander III," *Burlington Magazine*, No. 823, London, October 1971. – "Raoul Hausmann et Dada à Berlin," *Apeiros*, No. 6, Paris, Spring 1974. – "Collages," *Revue d'Esthétique*, Nos. 3/4, Collection 10/18, Paris 1978. – Marcos Ricardo BARNATAN, "Para una teoría del collage," *Guadalimar*, No. 46, Madrid 1979. – Garry APGAR, "Anch'io son pittore: Jean Huber, maître de la découpure," *Revue du Vieux-Genève*, Geneva 1986.

INDEX

LIST OF ILLUSTRATIONS

175

PRODUCED BY THE TECHNICAL STAFF OF
ÉDITIONS D'ART ALBERT SKIRA S.A., GENEVA

COLOUR AND BLACK AND WHITE,
FILMSETTING AND PRINTING BY
IRL IMPRIMERIES RÉUNIES LAUSANNE S.A.

BINDING BY H.+J. SCHUMACHER AG
SCHMITTEN (FRIBOURG)